AS I LIVE *and* BREATHE

AS I LIVE

BREATHE

notes of a patient-doctor

JAMIE WEISMAN, M.D.

NORTH POINT PRESS

A division of Farrar, Straus and Giroux

New York

North Point Press
A division of Farrar, Straus and Giroux
19 Union Square West, New York 10003

Distributed in Canada by Douglas & McIntyre Ltd.
Printed in the United States of America
First edition, 2002

Grateful acknowledgment is made for permission to reprint the following
material: "Rent," from *The Flashboat: Poems Collected and Reclaimed* by
Jane Cooper. Copyright © 2000 by Jane Cooper. Used by permission
of W. W. Norton & Company, Inc.
"Evening" by Rainer Maria Rilke, translated by Stephen Mitchell. From *The
Selected Poetry of Rainer Maria Rilke* by Rainer Maria Rilke,
translated by Stephen Mitchell, copyright © 1982 by Stephen Mitchell.
Used by permission of Random House, Inc.

Library of Congress Cataloging-in-Publication Data
Weisman, Jamie.
    As I live and breathe, notes of a patient-doctor / Jamie Weisman.
        p.   cm.
    ISBN 0-86547-602-0 (hc. : alk. paper)
    1. Weisman, Jamie—Health.   2. Immunological deficiency syndromes—
Patients—Georgia—Biography.   3. Physicians—Georgia—Biography.
I. Title.
RC606 . W45 2002
610'.92—dc21
[B]
                                                                    2001054378

Designed by Patrice Sheridan

www.fsgbooks.com

1   3   5   7   9   10   8   6   4   2

to victor

CONTENTS

AS I LIVE *and* BREATHE

INFUSION

In the infusion room at Mount Sinai Hospital, the chairs were a grayish-pink vinyl; they tilted back and the legs rose up, and you could go to sleep. The chairs had wide armrests, and the arms that rested there were pierced with needles leading back to hollow plastic tubes, through which dripped the clear viscous fluid that maintained the life of each person in each chair. A television and a VCR were suspended overhead. No one ever changed the channel, and it slipped from *Oprah* to news of an earthquake to the afternoon soaps in a drone not quite loud enough to be understood but better than silence.

When I started coming to the infusion room, I was

twenty-six years old, but I'd been sick for eleven years. It took that long to figure out how to treat me, and during that time I'd been to hospitals from Minnesota to Massachusetts. I'd had three operations, four lymph nodes removed, five bone marrow biopsies. I'd been called a hypochondriac by my boss and been told by a hematologist that I had or would soon have cancer. Finally a diagnosis was reached: some form of congenital immune deficiency, the exact nature of which is still unknown. I was prescribed interferon, to inject into the soft part of my belly or my thigh every other night, and I started going once a month to the infusion room, on the tenth floor of a building just off Fifth Avenue, to receive intravenous immunoglobulin.

I'm remembering a specific day as I write this essay, but all the days were pretty much the same. The patients settled into their chairs; some of us would bring lunch or juice. We'd greet each other and glance at the window, comment on the weather, extract from bags whatever we needed to entertain ourselves for a few hours: homework, crayons, newspapers, knitting. On the day I am thinking of, I was carrying my heavy general chemistry textbook and a problem set due at the end of the week. The other patients, already hooked up to IVs, dozed or read or stared into space. My friend Jane was there, reading from a book of Robert Lowell's poems—we'd been talking about him the month before. Another patient, Charlotte, had just come back from a trip to Hawaii, and she'd brought in pineapples for the nurses. Three-year-old Dovid was kneeling on the floor, one hand gripping a crayon, the other taped down to hold a needle and IV line in place. His mother watched him from a chair while she knit a sweater. And I was balancing chemical reactions because, after losing my health and then miraculously having it restored to me, I'd decided to go to medical school.

I was always glad to see Jane there, and I ignored my chemistry book to catch up with her. Sarah, the nurse, swabbed alcohol on my forearm to clean it for the IV, then waved her hand to dry it so the alcohol wouldn't sting. Jane read a line of a poem to me—"A father's no shield for his child"—and we started discussing Lowell and his mental illness and his daughter and parenthood. Out of the corner of my eye, I could see Sarah unwrapping the needle from its sterile packaging. An IV needle is much larger than the one used to draw blood. She tapped the vein with her gloved hand and whispered, "Little pinch."

The moment when one's skin is pierced produces a unique vulnerability that has nothing to do with pain. It is fundamentally unnatural to passively allow this insult to the body, and no matter how many times I've had it done to me, I still flinch. It is always when I feel the prick of the needle that the "why me?" thoughts come, as if they were smoke leaking out through the tiny hole in my arm. How did I end up with an aberrant immune system? Which one of my chromosomes misbehaved? Why would one of *my* cells mess up the intricate process of division, when trillions of other cells in billions of other people manage it just fine, thousands of times every hour? We—my doctors, my family, myself—have no idea where my disorder came from or where it is going. I could develop cancer next year, or I could, like my grandfather, die of old age at ninety while eating a Rice Krispies Treat and complaining about the weather. Sometimes when the needle slides into my vein, I am overwhelmed by this uncertainty.

It helped me to feel less sorry for myself if I talked while

my IV was being put in, and if Jane was there, I usually
talked to her. Jane had brittle gray-blond hair, cut in a page-
boy, and a small face with pale blue, almost clear eyes. She
had recently been named State Poet of New York. She had
also survived seventy years with an immune deficiency. Before she retired, she taught at Sarah Lawrence College, and
her students must have loved her. She had a natural love of
teaching and seemed genuinely thrilled by poetry. Jane and
I tried to schedule our appointments together so that we
could talk about poetry while, by the grace of Mount Sinai
and good health insurance, our bodies were given what they
lacked. The first time we met, at either my second or third
infusion, Jane had shown me a broadside of one of her poems, "Rent." It begins: "If you want my apartment, sleep in it
/ but let's have a clear understanding: the books are free
agents." I loved the idea that books could be free agents,
our loyalty to them not necessarily reciprocated. It's essentially a love poem, and it ends with a plea for "a radiance of
attention . . . a kind of awe / attending the spaces between
us— / Not a roof but a field of stars."

It made me think of Rilke's poem "Evening." As I'd gotten
sick, the poem had become more meaningful to me, and by
then I knew it by heart. Jane knew it, too. In the poem,
Rilke describes that silent moment at the end of day when
the sky darkens and the world seems to separate itself—the
constrained earth, the infinite sky—and we are left, "not at
home in either one, / not so still and dark as the darkened
houses, / not calling to eternity with the passion / of what
becomes a star each night, and rises."

We both recognized that the poems express similar sentiments, sentiments that resonate with a more sour pang for
those who live close to death. They are about a longing for
and a fear of limitlessness, and we—the patients in the infu-

sion room, along with those awaiting transplants of bone marrow or hearts or livers, those getting chemotherapy and losing hair, those trying to walk again and those waking from comas—know that our lives are as limited as stone. It is what lies beyond them that is limitless. Stories and poems comfort us because they, like our lives, have beginnings and ends. Stories conclude when the lovers are united or part, when the boat returns home, when the war is over. For every life on the planet, however, each story has the same ending, and each person has the same, often unarticulated longing expressed in Jane's and Rilke's poems: to become stars, to live in roofless houses, to find another chapter after the last page.

Sarah announced that the IV was in my vein. I didn't look while she threaded the needle. Instead, I asked Jane where she thought the rhythm of a poem comes from. A small drop of blood fell on my skin, the backward leak of the IV.

Jane answered, "Boom-*boom*. Boom-*boom*. From the heartbeat. To be. Boom-*boom*. Or not. Boom-*boom*. To be."

Sarah hooked the tube into the needle, and the immunoglobulin started dripping. "Here comes your juice," she said.

I looked around me at the other patients, at Charlotte's kind round face and Dovid's black eyes and long lashes, bent over the picture he was drawing, at Mike, an airplane mechanic, sleeping peacefully, and Bob, talking on his cell phone. It was almost impossible to take in what each of them, and all of us collectively, had endured while we remained, essentially, who we always were. Every one of us knew what it felt like to be put to sleep for surgery and the horrible sensation of waking from anesthesia, a stranger calling your name, the blur of lights in the recovery room, your body convulsing when the tube is pulled from your throat.

We knew what it was to wait for biopsy results, to be seen naked by nurses and doctors, to argue with insurance companies, to get sick from medication and to have to take it anyway. While the medication dripped into our arms, we discussed these things, along with movies and gossip, the ups and downs of romances and the accomplishments of children, new shoes and sweaters, trips to the shore, the first time we got sick, the day we were diagnosed, miscarriages, tumors, wedding plans. We coped. We endured. We ate our lunch.

Once she saw my IV was running well, Sarah sliced up the pineapple Charlotte had brought from Hawaii and passed out chunks, using gauze for napkins. It was a lovely yellow and so sweet.

All of us in the infusion room at Mount Sinai either lacked antibodies or had antibodies that did not work. When blood is donated, it is separated into a variety of components, including red blood cells, platelets, and antibodies. Antibodies themselves are proteins specifically designed to help protect us from invaders. They float through our blood and lymph, our tears and saliva, finding things that don't look as if they belong in the body and marking them for destruction. Once an antibody recognizes an invader, it attaches to it, as if planting a flag on its surface. The cells that are involved in destroying invaders recognize the attached antibody—or flag—and know that the target needs to be eliminated. The destroying cells, three more varieties of white blood cells called macrophages, natural killer cells, and cytotoxic T cells, then come and ingest the designated invader.

We in the infusion room were not like the boy in the plastic bubble who could make neither antibodies nor destroying cells. He was immunologically naked, a body there for the taking, by bacteria, viruses, fungi, parasites—whatever needed a home. We had other functioning components to our immune systems, such as T cells that could recognize and kill invaders, even those unmarked by antibodies, and white blood cells called neutrophils that could seize and destroy bacteria. Yet even so, our immune systems were weak, and we were profoundly susceptible to certain diseases: pneumonia, meningitis, sepsis, diarrhea, ear and throat infections. We'd all suffered from these in one form or another.

There is no way to teach the body to make good antibodies if it isn't prewired to do so. In desperate cases, bone marrow is transplanted in an attempt to give the patient early blood cells that know how to make functioning antibodies. All blood cells start from a common precursor in the bone marrow, which then responds to signals to become a certain kind of white or red blood cell. In bone marrow transplants, the patient's bone marrow is wiped out and replaced by these early cells from a healthy donor, in the hope that they'll then grow and turn into healthy, mature cells. In order for the body to accept the transplant, however, its own immune mechanisms must be destroyed. Many patients die from infection during this process. If they survive, sometimes the opposite problem ensues: the transplanted white blood cells think the body in which they live is foreign, and they attack. When this happens, the new immune system must be suppressed again. In effect, then, the treatment for immune deficiency winds up being more immune deficiency. It is far safer simply to give people like us someone else's antibodies.

Antibodies, also called immunoglobulins, can be extracted from whole blood because they weigh a different amount than white and red blood cells. Once extracted, the fluid is treated to prevent transmission of viruses, such as HIV and hepatitis B and C. It takes gallons of whole blood to make a few ounces of antibodies, and antibody transfusions are therefore very expensive. My monthly treatments, which are small since I am small—just over five feet and one hundred pounds—and do have some good antibodies, run about $2,000 a pop. Other patients pay up to $8,000 per treatment and must be treated every two weeks. The fare is hefty, but it transports a patient from certain death to good health. Almost all the patients in the infusion room worked. Without the transfusions, we would all have qualified for disability while we waited to die.

There are more than a hundred genetic varieties of immune deficiencies, and in each a different aspect of the immune system malfunctions. The most common form of inborn immune deficiency—and the diagnosis shared by most people in the infusion room—presents with low levels of antibodies. But there are other immune deficiencies in which the body makes antibodies but they cannot attach to a target or, once attached, the killing cells can't do their job. In my case, my body makes antibodies, but they don't function correctly, and I am at risk for a number of viral infections. Many of these infections are caused by everyday viruses, including the virus that causes the common cold. But what might cause the average healthy person seven to ten days of low-grade fever, runny nose, and cough, for me can become a chronic infection, or worse, death. Even more frightening, it is now known that many viral diseases cause cancer, and my inability to fight these ordinary predators drastically increases my risk of cancer. Antibodies alone are not enough to ward these threats off; I also have to give myself injections of interferon.

Interferon, like insulin, is a natural product of the body. It helps kill viruses and cancer cells. A healthy person makes her own interferon, and that interferon daily helps instruct the body to destroy cells that don't belong there. For some reason, the interferon I make doesn't work, so I flood my body with man-made interferon to do the job. The combination of interferon and antibodies was first developed to treat children who developed lymphoma as a result of a viral infection after having their immune systems destroyed to receive a bone marrow transplant. I have never had a bone marrow transplant, but my immune system resembles the damaged immune systems of those patients enough so that the treatment that worked for them has also worked, albeit imperfectly, for me. If you saw me in the street, you would have no idea that I was anything other than perfectly healthy. The same is true for most patients with inborn immune deficiencies. We gather in rooms monthly or weekly to receive transfusions, and only then, with IV catheters in our arms, do we appear different from other mothers and mechanics and teachers and lawyers and cab drivers and cashiers.

Prior to beginning treatment with immunoglobulin, I had repeated infections of the parotid gland, a large salivary gland that sits along the jaw. Such infections, called parotitis (*itis* just means "inflammation"), are exquisitely painful and make it almost impossible to eat, as food causes the salivary gland to contract, squirting out saliva. I'd survived the infections, but each one left some scar tissue, and after seven bouts of parotitis in the left gland, I had a heap of scar tissue just under the skin of my cheek that made me look as if I had a permanent case of one-sided mumps. Reassurances that the swelling was not noticeable were daily belied by the quizzical looks of strangers. Some people came out and asked me what had happened to my face, and an ex-boyfriend told me he didn't want to look at me because it made him sad. Him! I didn't share these petty sorrows with my doctor or my family. I shared them with the other patients in the infusion room, just as they shared theirs with me.

For many of us, the infusion room served as a sort of de facto therapy group, a place where we could share the burdens of our conditions—like my swollen face—without hurting family members or feeling that we were wasting our doctors' precious time. The position of the sick patient in the family is an awkward one. As much as your parents or husband or children might want you to come to them with your worries and pains, whatever you say only heightens their feelings of helplessness and anxiety, and often the patient ends up consoling the listener. Although we are at the mercy of our bodies, at least we are the ones *in* the bodies, and to whatever degree we can, we steer them. We take our medication, our vitamins; we sleep when we should; we show up for our infusions; we press on our lumps and bumps to see if they hurt or if they are growing. Our loved ones do not have this power. If they could have, my parents would have traded immune systems with me, but obviously this isn't an option. Instead, they bravely listen to my fears, accompany me on bone marrow biopsies, and watch their child suffer, not as penance but as a way of participating, as close to being in my body as they can get. At the same time, I am keenly aware of the pain I cause them merely by telling them I hurt, and so I experience the double agony of my own misfortune and theirs. As genuine as their desire is to share this whole sad process with me, it cannot overcome my desire to spare them, and so very little relief comes from talking to them about it.

As for doctors, no matter how patient they are, you see them only for a while, and inevitably you remember the most important question after they have left the room. Further, while they are interested in your symptoms and your subjective perception of your health, it feels inappropriate to share with them the quotidian and often nonmedical consequences of those problems.

When I got engaged, I went to visit Jane in her apartment up near Columbia University. I was no longer living in New York. I had started medical school in Atlanta, and I sorely missed the companionship of the infusion room. Jane had had a difficult winter. She had been hospitalized with severe diarrhea. Her immune deficiency was to blame for that, but not for the worsening Parkinson's disease that kept her locked in her apartment, sorting through old manuscripts with stiffening arms that moved with the stops and starts of a tin soldier. She had lost a great deal of weight, and her skin had become tender, almost translucent. Her blue eyes looked even bigger in her face, as if they were pools gathering water, flooding.

Jane recognized immediately the mix of guilt and joy I felt at asking another human being to share in the ambiguity of my life. I credit my husband with tremendous courage in loving me, someone whose future is from the start more fragile than others'. I could leave him alone with children to raise; I could condemn him to nursing me through a painful, drawn-out illness. Although I am not expecting such tragedies, I have to recognize that I'm at greater risk for them than the average thirty-year-old. Jane had never wanted anyone to take on the burden of loving her, given her poor health, and she'd never married. Such deep regrets patients rarely share with their doctors and cannot share with their families. We share them with each other, not expecting resolution but just the relief of genuine, unmitigated empathy.

Three years ago I put on a black robe with a green sash and was graduated from medical school. My experience with disease had inspired me to go there, and my monthly trips to the infusion center were as essential to my medical education as any course in anatomy or physiology. The patients I met shaped the doctor I would become. I know illness from the inside out. I know not just what goes wrong in the body—how the white cells start to divide out of control in leukemia, how the heart weakens in congestive heart failure, how blood clots clog the arteries in stroke victims—but also what this means for the human being who happens to inhabit a given body. I learned part of this myself, through experience, but most of it I was taught by the patients in the infusion center who were my teachers and my friends.

In Atlanta, where I now live and receive infusions, the infusion room is laid out differently. Emory University does not have an area devoted to immunodeficiencies. Instead its large infusion center is broken up into four smaller areas with about eight chairs each, to give the patients privacy. As at Mount Sinai, the room is set up to be as comfortable as possible. The nurses know us all by name, and there are snacks—fluorescent orange cheese crackers with peanut butter—and sodas. On Friday mornings, a local church drops off fruit and muffins. Everyone who needs an infusion goes there. Most are cancer patients, getting their chemotherapy or replacing what's been wiped out of their bone marrow—red blood cells or platelets. Other patients, like me, have more obscure diagnoses: Waldenström's macroglobulinemia, scleroderma, Sjögren's syndrome, histiocytosis X. Now that I've finished medical school, I know what all those names mean, what diseases they describe, but you cannot know what they are as an *illness* until you see them in a patient.

Just about everyone I saw regularly in the infusion room knew I was a medical student, and they took pride in educating me about the subtleties of their conditions. Nora described her battle with chronic leg ulcers. "Nothing works," she said, "not bandages, not keeping them elevated, not blood thinners." Every time I saw her, she rolled up her pants to show the wounds and instructed me, "Find a cure for this while you're at it." Diane had uveitis, inflammation deep in the eye that makes sunlight horribly painful. She told me, "I know it's coming when I wake up feeling like there's an ice chip in my eye. By that afternoon, it's flaming red." I knew what I was supposed to look for to diagnose uveitis, but the ice chip was news. These patients did not just show me the full human dimension of their illness, which was obvious. They actually taught me, in words much clearer than textbooks, what their diseases felt like, looked like, even smelled like. Nora said, "I can't stand it. My feet smell like defrosting steak."

On the day I met Brian, he told me he was scheduled for surgery because he had "a touch of brain cancer," but he said it didn't bother him too much. To an observer, all the patients in the infusion room seem astonishingly brave, but what choice do we have? We know what the alternative is: self-pity, debilitating fear.

I could have been the one wheeling Brian into the operating room when I was on my anesthesiology rotation. I told him to make sure to ask for Zofran, a drug that makes patients less nauseated after anesthesia. We agreed that the nausea was as bad as the pain. When I stand over a patient, post-op, most would never suspect that I know exactly what they feel. I've been told by surgeons and anesthesiologists that you forget the pain immediately following an operation. They're wrong. And pain changes you. Your mind and your body temporarily become enemies, and your body has a strong advantage. When you hurt, you can't do anything but hurt, and so, after pain, you know that the part of you that thinks and loves, reads and wonders, laughs and remembers, is at the mercy of the part of you that breathes.

Some of the patients saved questions for me that they were embarrassed to ask their doctors, though the questions were never stupid. Who needs white blood cells, anyway? How come I'm at risk for a stroke just because I have lupus? I tried to help them, but in fact we helped each other. Jennifer had lymphoma, and she was scheduled for a cord bone marrow transplant. She was nervous, and Patsy, who was two months post-transplant, warned her that she would feel pretty awful from all the chemo before the transplant, but afterward—she stood up and twirled—"Well, look at me!" She took off her wig. "My hair's even growing back!" I thought of them when I was on my dermatology rotation, watching a lip biopsy on a bone marrow transplant patient, done to assess the success of the transplant. I stayed in the room, and I knew, when the patient started to cry because she was having difficulty holding the numbing liquid in her mouth, that it was not because of this one difficulty. It was because of months and months of pain, sickness, and uncertainty. Our diseases overwhelm us at the strangest times. One patient told me that when it was all over and she was in remission, she found herself crying in the grocery store as she tried to choose a jar of jelly for her son's sandwiches.

Once in a while, of course, someone stops coming to one of the infusion rooms. This is almost never because he or she is cured. The infusion room is a place for people with chronic illnesses, diseases medicine has learned how to manage but not to correct. On the day I am remembering, six years ago in the infusion room in New York City, I was studying for my third general chemistry exam. I had not been hospitalized in a year. I was running, skiing. I had energy, and I felt that I could take on medical school. That morning the Oscar nominations had been announced, and we debated who was going to win. Jane's book of poetry, *Maps and Windows*, was being reissued. We were eating pineapple straight from Hawaii, and little Dovid finished a picture for one of the nurses and signed it in a scrawl with his free hand. Outside the window, gray smoke curled on the roof of a yellowed building. Taxicabs honked. Water towers reflected the slate sky. But there was sad news. MaryAnne had died.

She had been one of the sickest patients in the infusion room. I never knew her diagnosis, but I knew that she could barely eat. She received intravenous feeds and supplemental nutrients, and she was still skeletal. Her eyeglasses took up all of her face, and her deflated lips were almost invisible, as if she'd swallowed them. Her son was also immune deficient, and they used to receive their immunoglobulin together, holding hands. We all knew that any of us could become MaryAnne, and we all thought this together, Jane and I, Charlotte and Dovid's mother, though mercifully not Dovid. The pineapple we were eating could slip through our bowels undigested; our blood could thin and pool in our wrists and ankles. We might one day require permanent catheters to receive our antibody transfusions, and we could pour gallons of the stuff into our veins and it still wouldn't work. It wouldn't be enough anymore, and we would die.

In all our discussions, Jane and I never really commented on the irony of discussing fiction—made-up stories—amid the real life-and-death drama going on around us. It is easier, after all, to discuss Hamlet's death than that of someone you know—or, for that matter, your own.

The trickiest part of living is pretending that you don't know how the story ends. All of us in the infusion room have been too close to the last page to effectively feign that ignorance. The carriage has drawn up before the house; the bags are packed. The hero is descending the staircase. Even if we don't read the last line, we know that he leaves. We leave. All of us leave. Infusion rooms are unique because in these small, sterile places are gathered a disparate group of men and women who know this truth and live anyway— laugh, learn chemistry, write poems, plant gardens, read books anyway.

Jane asked how Aaron, MaryAnne's son, was holding up. Sarah answered, "He's okay. He's tough. And he's smart. We've arranged for him to get his infusions at home for a while."

MaryAnne's death at once touched me and left me cold. I barely knew her, and yet we shared an experience that I don't share with any of the people closest to me. Apparently, we were told, she was ready. She'd made arrangements for Aaron. There was a will. People with chronic conditions usually deteriorate slowly, though at the end there is often a crescendo, a sudden slipping and spilling when things break down rapidly and infection builds on infection, and there's a terrible racket in the body.

No one spoke. On the television overhead, two young soap opera lovers embraced. They appeared to be made of plastic. The drops of fluid in my IV glistened like diamonds. They dripped at a steady rhythm, the same boom-*boom* of my heartbeat as each squeeze of the muscle pushed blood through the vein, scooping up the new fluid as it passed. The same boom-*boom* of *Hamlet* and *Romeo and Juliet* and *The Tempest*. There *is* a rhythm of life, a long, extended poem, but it isn't loud enough for us to hear the words, just the drumming. We in the infusion room, and all the chronically ill and struggling patients all over the world, are closer to the sound than others are, but even we hear only a murmur, nothing distinct, no answers.

THE WAVES IN JAPAN

any man's death diminishes me,
because i am involved in mankind.

——john donne

Frank Hamilton was as close to death as the living get. His hollow face was trimmed with coarse, stringy gray hair that fell to his shoulders. It was the kind of hair you'd put on a monster mask. His lips were thin and almost colorless. There was no fat under the skin on his face; you could see the shape of his skull under his ashen cheeks. His eyes were pink and bloodshot, dug deep as if they'd been ground in with a thumb. Every bone in his hand was visible, the sharp splay of them, and his chest was so emaciated that the flat bones of his sternum stood out, and under them you could see the frantic trill of his heart.

He was in the last stages of alcoholism. He knew he was

dying. He'd known, he said, for at least a year, but he had not been able to quit drinking. He had tried medication, Alcoholics Anonymous, church programs, programs sponsored by the Veterans Administration. He had been sober for long stretches at a time, months, close to a year once, but he always went back to drinking.

Mr. Hamilton was a patient at the Atlanta VA hospital, where I was assigned during my second month of internship. These hospitals have a reputation for being understaffed and underfunded, but the hospital where I was working had recently been renovated, with a state-of-the-art intensive care unit and new operating rooms. The patient rooms, however, were still the old quads, four people to a room, their beds separated only by a thin pink curtain.

When I first entered the hospital, I had been stunned by the number of amputees. At every corner, I passed men on crutches and in wheelchairs, awkwardly maneuvering the stumps of their legs through the hallways. They were, I assumed, casualties of war. It turned out that most of them had lost their legs not to grenades or land mines but to poorly controlled diabetes and to cigarettes. Toxins from cigarette smoke cause scarring and shrinking of the blood vessels, which cuts off the blood supply to the limb. The majority of heart and vascular disease at the VA was self-inflicted through tobacco.

At the end of my month of working there, I looked back over my list of patients and saw that I had cared for forty-eight patients. All but two contributed to their own diseases through smoking and/or drinking. I had diagnosed two men with terminal lung cancer. Each had smoked at least two packs a day for at least thirty years. I had sent five men for heart surgery, one of them just thirty-eight years old. Two others had died: one from throat cancer, which simply is not seen in people who don't smoke or chew tobacco, and one from heart failure (he died with a pack of cigarettes in his shirt pocket). I had two alcoholics, who were clearly suffering the effects of their alcoholism, but almost all my patients drank to some degree. One of the alcoholics told me he drank to forget the fact that he was an alcoholic. He laughed when he said it, but there seemed to be more than a little truth in the statement. The other alcoholic was Frank Hamilton.

Americans spend billions of dollars each year treating the effects of drinking and smoking. Most patients I have met know exactly what they are doing to themselves. They have been told by their doctors that the smoking and the drinking will kill them. Still, they persist. They sit in wheelchairs in the VA smoking area, their throats cut away to remove cancers, and smoke cigarettes through the tracheostomy holes in their necks. Caring for patients who persist in damaging their bodies is inevitably frustrating. To give chemotherapy to treat lung cancer in a patient who is still smoking feels futile. It reminds me of a children's poem in which an old woman continuously rakes smooth the waves in the ocean: useless and absurd.

These addictions in the face of the obvious deterioration of a patient's health are difficult for me to understand, since I don't smoke and rarely drink. I'm sick enough without further abusing my body. Little by little, my disease seeps into more and more of my life. Small knots of scar tissue are forming under the skin of my belly from my interferon shots. Some nights my entire body aches from the side effects of the shot. I sweat through my pajamas. I have to carry bottles of eyedrops with me wherever I go since my eyes cannot make tears. The tear glands have been destroyed by white blood cells: the same cells that fail in their job of protecting me from infection have turned around and attacked my own body. Every day I must pack eyedrops and medications with ice packs before I walk out of the house. Every month I go to the infusion room. If there were something I could give up, something I could stop doing, to make all this go away, wouldn't I do it in a heartbeat? Wouldn't I never have another glass of wine, another cup of coffee, another chocolate bar, ice-cream cone, strawberry? There isn't any food or other substance I love enough that I wouldn't sacrifice it to have my health back. And so for me to see otherwise healthy men and women cripple themselves is sad, baffling, and infuriating.

By the time I met him, Mr. Hamilton had been admitted to the hospital at least ten times for severe bleeding, from the veins around his esophagus and from alcohol-induced ulcers in his stomach. Once he had torn a blood vessel while vomiting after drinking too much and had bled profusely. This is how Jack Kerouac died, vomiting blood from ruptured varicose veins in his esophagus, the classic drunk's death. On his current admission, Mr. Hamilton was bleeding both from ulcers and from the torn veins.

Mr. Hamilton had advanced cirrhosis, which meant that his liver was about half the size of a normal liver. Cirrhosis is a fancy word for scarring of the liver, and it results from years of exposure to toxic levels of alcohol. When something scars, it shrinks and turns hard. A healthy liver feels like a sopping sponge. A cirrhotic liver has the consistency of firm rubber, like a tire. Scarring of the liver causes all the other problems associated with alcoholism: bleeding, swollen legs and abdomen, confusion, shaking, insanity, coma, and death.

Because a severely scarred liver cannot make protein to thicken the blood, fluid seeped from Mr. Hamilton's blood vessels, swelling his belly like an enormous balloon. Yet years of malnutrition—"liquid lunches"—had atrophied his arms and legs, so that his knees were wider than his thighs and his elbows bigger than his biceps. He walked, when he could walk, with the swaybacked, hands-on-hips walk of a woman in her ninth month of pregnancy. As he got weaker, he could not muster this stance. He bought a cane and walked hunched forward with his belly hanging low like an udder. On his last admission to the hospital, he was too exhausted even for this kind of walking, and he requested a wheelchair. He was forty-eight years old.

Mr. Hamilton required drainage of his abdominal fluid every other week. It is not only uncomfortable but quite dangerous to accumulate fluid in the belly. As the abdomen fills up, the fluid pushes up on the diaphragm, compressing the lungs and decreasing the ability to breathe. When respiration is compromised, we drain the fluid in a simple procedure known as paracentesis, which involves inserting a large piece of rubber tubing into the abdomen and allowing the fluid to drain into a bag. Most of us have little or no free fluid in our abdomens. Mr. Hamilton, I estimated, had more than four gallons, over thirty pounds.

The fluid comes out a pale, red-tinged yellow, translucent unless it's infected. You collect it in a thick plastic bag with lines to mark the liters. Since the patient can pass out during the procedure, I had to stay with Mr. Hamilton while we drained his belly, a slow process given the amount we were removing. And so we had time—hours at a stretch—to talk. I knew more about him than I have known about almost any other patient, but I really knew nothing. I certainly never knew why he drank—if he was trying to forget somebody or something, whether it was something he'd started and just couldn't stop, compelling as a love affair, or whether he simply liked it, as another alcoholic had answered me when I asked him why he consumed three to four pints of vodka a day.

This is what I did know: He was stateside during the Vietnam War. He did not enlist; he served because he was drafted. He had trained as an architect. For a time, he'd been a professional classical guitarist and had adapted some of the compositions of Bach, Schoenberg, and Brahms to the instrument. He had lived in Japan for several years, in a small town, and he had caught fish from Japanese waters and made it into sashimi, which he preferred to sushi. I pictured him in a small Japanese house with sliding translucent rice paper doors, sitting with his knees tucked under him, barefoot at a table. He spoke fluent Japanese, and I asked him to say something for me. He muttered a few sharp, twangy syllables and smiled grimly. I asked him what he had said.

" 'Thank you for helping me.' "

"You're welcome," I answered.

The fluid ballooned the bag out. When I felt it, it was warm, the temperature of the body, which human hands know subconsciously by touch.

He muttered something else in Japanese, but when I asked him what he'd said that time, he wouldn't tell me. He just shook his head. Then he craned up to look at his belly, draped in sterile blue paper. He pressed tentatively on it. "Sometimes I think I could just put a pin in it and pop it."

One morning I walked in to find an attractive blond woman in Bermuda shorts and a headband sitting at his bedside.

She stood up to shake my hand and introduced herself as his wife. There was a shocking disparity in the way the two of them looked. Everybody appeared to be bursting with health compared to Mr. Hamilton, but his wife seemed to glow. I wondered how she'd stood by, a woman in seeming perfect health, gainfully employed, and watched him deteriorate. Outside the room, she confided that he was still drinking. "But he's going to stop now," she said. "Frank wants a liver transplant." She folded her hands around her purse. "He knows now how serious it is."

I didn't say at the time—nor did I ever say—that not one single doctor caring for her husband, including the chief of medicine, thought he had a chance of getting a transplant. Alcoholics can get liver transplants; all they have to do is stop drinking. Alcoholics and drug users are considered for transplant if they can show six months of documented abstinence. Some people in medicine disagree with this policy. They do not believe that patients whose actions ruined their organs should be eligible for transplant. It is hard to get past the idea that destroying one's liver by drinking is a voluntary act. Shouldn't the innocent bystanders, those struck with liver cancer or other diseases, have first crack at the limited number of livers that we have? But medicine has chosen not to judge. We do not know the origins of addiction, and so we do not consider how your liver was destroyed, only how you'll take care of the new one, the gift.

Mr. Hamilton still denied that he was drinking, except for the occasional glass of wine, but random blood alcohol tests found him to be as much as six times over the legal limit. Because he was bleeding all the time, his doctors, including myself, felt that unless something was done to clear up the congestion in his scarred liver, Mr. Hamilton would die within months, either from bleeding to death or from an inability to breathe or from kidney failure. The procedure that was suggested to Mr. Hamilton is a new one, a transjugular intrahepatic portosystemic shunt, or TIPS, as we call it.

We used to relieve a blockage in the liver by a major operation, opening up the patient's abdomen and reconnecting the main vein from the liver, the portal vein, to the superior vena cava, the vein that returns blood to the heart from the upper body, via a synthetic shunt. This connection creates a route for blood to flow around rather than through the liver. It is a bloody and intricate surgery. The veins are large: the portal vein is as big around as a quarter, the superior vena cava as a half dollar. Blood flow to the liver is interrupted during the procedure. Sewing the blood vessels to the shunt must be done perfectly or the connection will leak, resulting in hemorrhage.

Most cirrhotics are already very sick, and few can survive such major surgery. In the TIPS procedure, a radiologist can float a catheter down from the jugular vein in the neck to the liver and, jabbing with a needle, cut a path straight through the scarred organ. This connection relieves the traffic jam. There is no need to cut open the abdomen, and the patient is asleep for less time and has a greater chance of surviving.

In theory Mr. Hamilton could respond beautifully to the procedure, regain his strength long enough to quit drinking, and try for a liver transplant. In reality the gastroenterologists had largely given up. They'd gotten the random blood alcohol screens, all of which had been positive despite his professions of sobriety. They knew Mr. Hamilton was dying. The transjugular shunt was the only thing left to offer, so they offered it, but they did not believe it would help very much, if at all. It is hard for doctors to offer nothing but comfort, especially when even that offer may not be sincere.

Mr. Hamilton killed himself with alcohol, and if the point of being drunk is oblivion, he was just about there.

Mr. Hamilton was informed of the risks and benefits of the proposed TIPS procedure. Patients with liver failure cannot clot blood well and have difficulty maintaining adequate blood pressures. He was at risk for hemorrhage, which might result in heart and kidney failure and brain damage. Even if he did not bleed to death while on the table, the success of the procedure carried a new risk. With blood bypassing the portal vein, the liver cannot do its job, which includes removing toxins from the blood. As these toxins build up, the patient may become psychotic or even comatose. Further, if too much blood bypasses the liver, the organ may be deprived of oxygen and start to die—a condition called "shock liver" because it was first noted in patients in shock. It seemed an appropriate term for a TIPS patient: I could imagine their stunned and horrified livers gasping for breath, shocked at this sudden insult.

I explained all of this to Mr. Hamilton. I explained it again to his wife. I also explained that there was a good chance, even if he entered treatment, that he would not live the six months necessary to prove sobriety. I did not add that all of his doctors were almost certain he would be dead within six months. Mr. Hamilton thought carefully about it and drew up a list of questions, written in a shaky hand on notebook paper. What is the death rate? What is the long-term survival? Would it affect his chances for a transplant in the future?

"What would you do?" he kept asking me.

I told him that I did not know. I wanted no responsibility for this decision or its consequences.

Mr. Hamilton debated the procedure. Some days he was ready to go ahead; others he thought of checking out of the hospital and going home. Cirrhosis develops gradually, and so the patient gradually becomes adjusted to his limitations. He doesn't notice his sunken eyes, his thinned skin, his skeletal arms, because he has looked in the mirror every day, and one day is not that different from the one before. If you showed him a picture of himself five years ago, he would be stunned. But now he was accustomed to his weakness, to his protruding belly, to a life structured by doctor's visits. He was used to not working, to living on disability, to a cane and then a wheelchair. He wanted to know how much longer he could live this way. He wanted to know if the procedure was necessary to save his life. No one could answer these questions.

When Mr. Hamilton finally decided to go through with the procedure, he asked me if I thought it was a good idea. I ducked the question. "It's your decision."

"Will I still be able to get a transplant?"

I assured him that he could if he could stop drinking. Again, I did not tell him that with his advanced disease, the possibility of transplant was almost nonexistent. There was some part of me that wanted to see Mr. Hamilton give up alcohol. I wanted to see him quit. Maybe I wanted to see that this disease, alcoholism, unlike cancer, could be beaten with the mind alone. I wanted to know how strong his will was. Or maybe I wanted him to acknowledge his role in destroying his body, and how easy it would have been not to. Most patients are helpless victims of disease, old age, or, like myself, some genetic malfunction. There is no single thing we can do to cure ourselves. There was a point when all Mr. Hamilton had to do was stop drinking. Very few problems in life are that simple. If you dig deeper, alcoholism is not simple either, but for those who are not addicted, it seems so easy. You don't have to change your diet; you don't have to exercise; just lay off the booze. It is maddening to watch, and maybe I dangled that liver in front of Mr. Hamilton, dangled it across six months of sobriety, knowing full well he'd never reach it, because I was frustrated with him for refusing so simple a solution for his disease when I don't have one for my own.

The morning of Mr. Hamilton's procedure, I had to remove as much fluid as possible from his abdominal cavity. With gallons of fluid in the abdomen, the liver would have a tendency to bounce and float as the radiologists jabbed it. Less fluid, less floating. In order to insure that fluid from the blood did not rush into his abdomen to replace the fluid we were removing, we thickened Mr. Hamilton's blood with 50 grams of a protein, albumin. At fifty dollars a gram, that came to $2,500. Then we waited for the belly to deflate. Mr. Hamilton had also been in the hospital for a total of two weeks stabilizing and preparing for his procedure, at a cost of $500 per day. In the end, I estimated the total cost of his hospitalization, including five days in the intensive care unit, the procedure itself, and the expensive blood products and medications given, to come to about $25,000.

Mr. Hamilton and I talked to pass the time. He wanted to know how I'd ended up a doctor. Most doctors don't discuss their personal lives with their patients. As a patient as well as a doctor, I'm divided on the wisdom of this practice. On the one hand, it can be a burden to have to recognize your doctor's humanity, that doctors are fallible and have desires outside of caring for your health. After all, if you are sick, the last thing you want to hear about is your doctor's problems.

On the other hand, maybe we'd have a more egalitarian exchange if the doctor's fallibility could be recognized. Mr.

Hamilton sometimes seemed to feel that I knew the correct course of action and simply wouldn't tell him. I explained to him that doctors caring for patients with advanced disease almost always reach a point where we simply don't know what is best for the patient: to continue treatment or to let him die in peace, to cut him open or to offer morphine and a hospice bed. Still, he asked me every day what to do, and every day I told him that I did not know. With our greater knowledge of disease, our obscure vocabulary, our neutral talk of life and death, it is easy for doctors to appear omniscient and omnipotent rather than the common human beings we are, complete with desires, regrets, fears, and conflicts.

I told him that I'd been very sick myself at one point. That I'd been struggling to make it as a writer in New York City when the fact of my illness struck me. I needed health insurance. But why medicine? I needed a real job with a reliable income, and I knew no happy lawyers. My father was a doctor, and I'd unwittingly learned a lot of medicine in the course of my own disease, so I went to medical school. If I'd been a successful writer, selling screenplays with enough points to qualify for the Writers Guild health care plan, I probably wouldn't be standing at his bedside, my hands in sterile gloves, watching clear fluid drip into his vein while yellow-red fluid streamed out of his belly. I wouldn't be hearing him ask me if I thought he was going to die and then just as quickly telling me not to answer that question. I wouldn't be seeing him sweep his paper-thin eyelids shut against the thought that this morning, spent discussing life's disappointments with a near stranger, could be his last on earth.

The burly transporters, all in white, came to lift Mr. Hamilton onto his stretcher. He said nothing as he left. His wife

did not want to be in the hospital the morning of the procedure. She left her pager number with a nurse. A gray-haired
woman from his church helped me load his belongings into
a paper grocery bag—his slippers, his eyeglasses, a bag of
Gummi Bears—and push it with his newly issued wheelchair to intensive care, where he would go if he lived.

There is a basic premise in medicine that each life is priceless and that every life is worth saving. When we hold true
to this promise, we see medicine at its best: humble, rever-
ent, above and outside of commerce. Patients are not
judged; all human beings are treated equally: homeless or
CEO, illegal alien or movie star. We are all linked by the
common needs and functions of our bodies, and it is these
needs alone that are the concern of the doctor.

Of course, in practice such ideals are impossible to maintain. In America, more than in any other industrialized country, access to health care is determined by finances, class,
education, race, age, and employment. HMOs determine
which medication, operation, or radiation should be available to the patient. There is a shortage of medical resources,
not only of transplant organs but also of specialists and
equipment, in rural areas and in ghettos. We have achieved
more in medicine than we can afford to give, and all our
new discoveries come with a price tag: $200,000 for a liver
transplant, $50,000 for neurosurgery, $2,000 a day for a bed
in the intensive care unit, $12 to vaccinate a child against
tetanus.

Researchers in Oregon actually attempted to determine a
price at which it was worth saving a life. They estimated that
up to $30,000 per year of life saved was a worthwhile ex-
penditure. So one million dollars spent on a premature baby

in the neonatal ICU is a bargain, since in theory it saves up to seventy-two years of life, the average life span, which, by these calculations, is worth over two million dollars. On the other hand, the $15,000 spent trying to save my eighty-seven-year-old grandfather after he fell and bruised his brain was a waste, since he died. And as for my own life? My infusions cost about $2,000 a month and my interferon shots another $300, so the bill for my medicine alone comes to about $28,000 a year. I am fortunate to have multiple health insurance policies to help me pay for all of this. This year I have been hospitalized twice and have had one major operation, so my medical expenses may reach $50,000. Am I stealing from society?

There are certainly times when I consider the needs of the world and wonder if my life is indeed worth this huge expenditure. I am subsidized by all the other people who share my insurance policy, and I wonder how many of these strangers would voluntarily offer this money to keep me alive. Every life is priceless, as long as no one gets the bill. You might compare my life to Mr. Hamilton's and argue that I did not cause my disease and am therefore more deserving of care. But we do not know why some people become alcoholics, any more than we know why my immune system does not work properly. You might say there is more value in my life because I pay taxes, because I am a doctor and I help people. Yet for every applicant accepted to medical school, ten more are turned down, thousands of perfectly healthy people willing and able to do my job, pay my taxes, feed my dog, live, on the surface of it, my life. You can apply the same reasoning to all my patients: to Nicholas, an eleven-year-old who developed brain damage after a viral infection and required two years of hospitalization and rehabilitation, or to sixty-two-year-old Jack Reynolds, who nearly smoked his heart to death and just had bypass surgery. Both recovered. Who knows what Nicholas will do with his life: Find a cure for cancer? Become a sports announcer, teach kindergarten, deal drugs, die tomorrow in a boating accident? How will we know if we've recouped our investment? Mr. Reynolds has been on disability for two years already, having lost a leg to diabetes. Even after the surgery, he won't work again. He lives alone, estranged from his wife and children, and mostly watches television. His surgery was paid for by your taxes. Was it worth it?

On the other extreme are those who value human life infinitely. On pediatrics I met a child whose brain had slipped down through the hole in her skull into her neck. A team of neurosurgeons had heroically saved her life. Life alone was all that was left. She was paralyzed, wheeled around in a special chair that adapted to her contracted arms and legs. She had seizures every few minutes, in which her small brown eyes—which could not see since they were not connected to the visual cortex in her brain—would suddenly tremble in their sockets like shaken marbles, then stop. It costs about the same amount to keep that child alive as it does to keep me alive. Is her life any less valuable than mine? Is a year in the life of an alcoholic, which will be spent drinking and vomiting—or of a baseball player, a lawyer, a gardener, a stockbroker, a cab driver—worth more or less?

These issues of whom to treat and how much to spend are all abstract until you apply them to an individual life. To my fellow residents, they're something to debate on off-call nights over a pitcher of beer. To me, they are the difference between life and death. If I were to lose my health insurance, the cost of my medical care would exceed by at least ten thousand dollars the after-tax income I have as a resident. I would have to go on Medicaid, in which case I could not own a car or a house (such possessions would disqualify me); Medicaid might or might not pay for all my treatments. If the government or an insurance company chose not to pay, I would die. My very existence, along with the existence of millions of other patients, is thus reduced to finances.

Cogent arguments can be made either way—we should care for all people, or we should create a set of rules to determine whose life is worth saving or how much is worth spending. But these arguments demand consistency, and few of us can produce it.

Meanwhile, in the luxury of a government hospital, I could expend all possible resources to extend the life of Mr. Hamilton—architect, musician, Vietnam veteran, husband, and alcoholic. We took him to the interventional radiology suite to carve the shunt into his liver. There, wearing bright blue lead aprons to protect their reproductive organs, in a room lit by the glow of television screens, the radiologists, one eye on the body, one eye on the screen, watched a catheter float down through the dark lines of Mr. Hamilton's veins. The inferior vena cava, the largest vein in the body, is about the width of a Coke bottle. To visualize it, dye is injected so that it shows up on the screen as an inky blush. When the dye reaches the liver, it spreads out like a river with its tributaries. Beneath the unsteady stops and starts of the human hand advancing the catheter are the very regular, reliable pulsations of the heart. It is all visible on the television screen, the bulky triangle of the liver, the dark ragged lines of veins, the rhythm of the patient's life, slowed and dampened with anesthesia to a series of dull thuds. Once in the hepatic vein, the doctors stabbed at the liver a few times until they hit the portal vein. Then blood rushed from the fat portal vein into the hepatic vein, which swelled with the new load. A metal stent was placed in the new shunt to keep it open. And then it was over.

When I saw Mr. Hamilton next, he was in the intensive care unit. He was still intubated, and the clear plastic tube hung out of his mouth, distorting it into a crushed O. There was dried blood around his lips. The tube distended his cheek, stretching the thin skin so the harsh light of the room shone right through his face. His blue eyes were open, but he could not talk. He was so frail, it seemed a strong wind could blow him away—except that his wrists were tied to the bed's railing to prevent him from pulling the tube out of his mouth in his postanesthesia confusion. His eyes widened when I came into the room. I told him first that he was alive. Other patients have told me that when they first come out of anesthesia, there is a moment when they aren't quite certain of this fact. He strained to look at me, and his lips closed around the tube in his mouth. "You can't talk now," I said, "but we'll get the tube out soon. The surgery went fine. Everything is fine."

I called his wife and left a message that the procedure had gone well. Later they took the tube out of his throat, and he was able to breathe on his own. The next morning he was stable, and honoring a request he'd made prior to surgery, he was transferred out of intensive care to a room with three other patients. He was still very weak, but he was able to nod and mumble to questions, and when the nurse came with his medicine, he sat up in bed and let the pills rattle down his throat. We were waiting. We were waiting for the shunt to start working. We were waiting for his belly to shrink. Or we were waiting for the side effects: confusion, insanity, coma, bleeding, death.

Usually insanity descends unexpectedly. I asked Mr. Hamilton the basic questions: his name, his age, the year and month and day. I asked him where we were, and he answered, "The VA hospital," flatly, without relief. He did not smile or object. He was an intelligent man, and he knew that I was asking these questions to see if he was slipping away from consciousness into delirium. By his answers, at least the first day, I judged him to be still among us.

The next morning he was lost. I found him in his bed, in the corner of the room. No one had noticed that he was mumbling to himself and his hands were shaking. Large bruises like spilled paint spread out over his forearms and legs. The nurses had tied him to the bed because the night before he'd fallen trying to get to the bathroom by himself.

His mouth was moving automatically, up and down, like a doll's, not forming any sounds. There was still some dried, cracked blood etching his lips, darkened to black. His transparent skin, loosely wrapped around his body, was turning yellow, not a sunny lemon yellow but the musty, dirty color of old paper. Even the smell of him was changing, sour over sweet and old; he had a nursing-home smell. When I said his name, there was no flicker of recognition on his face. I held up his arms and pushed back on his fingers, and they flapped forward, as if he were trying, fraily, to play patty-cake. This hand flapping is called asterixis, and it is known to occur when ammonia, a toxic by-product of protein and the principal toxin that the liver removes, accumulates in the body. Asterixis has been observed in dying men since ancient Greek times, and I was joining a long line of physicians in observing it now.

The shunt had not worked, and Mr. Hamilton's liver was dying. I sat at the nurses' station writing down lab values from the computer. Every one of the measures of liver function and health were terribly abnormal. The protein clotting factors in his blood were down; he could not maintain his blood pressure. Liver cells were dying. Bilirubin was accumulating, giving his face the ashy yellow color. His urine was dark brown, there was blood in his stools, and still his belly was swollen up and about to pop.

The gastroenterology fellow came looking for Mr. Hamilton's chart. When I showed him the list of labs, he scanned down the computer screen and concluded, "He's dying now."

"Can't we undo the shunt?" I asked.

The fellow gestured at my list of lab values. "He'd bleed to death if we tried that now." He shook his head. "This happens sometimes, and they die. You knew he was going to die soon, didn't you?"

I knew. But *soon* and *now* are not the same thing, especially to the person who is dying.

When I went back into Mr. Hamilton's room later, his friend from church, who had helped me pack up his belongings two days before, was sitting by his bed. She was a proper gray-haired woman, who spoke with the wry, clear enunciation of a New England matron. She sat very straight in a blue vinyl chair she'd dragged out of the waiting room. Mr. Hamilton was groaning and tugging weakly at his restraints, not really making an effort to get free, as if he knew at this point that there was nowhere to go to escape death.

Mr. Hamilton's friend was holding his cane in one hand, and for no clear reason she said, "You know, Frank had invented a new kind of tent. We were going to market it ourselves. He was very excited about this. It is really a marvelous tent."

We both watched him struggle on the bed for a minute. I said, "Things don't look good."

She nodded. "Clearly." She placed the cane against the bed. "I don't think I'll have the energy to sell that tent on my own."

Mr. Hamilton died that night, and all his ideas, for harmonies and tunes and tents, all the old injuries that lived on in his memory, died with him. I felt terrible, but my feelings were complicated. He was my first patient to die, a milestone in my career as a doctor. Objectively, all he had lost was a few months of life. What difference would a few months of life have made in his condition, debilitated and in pain as he was? Yet I knew he wanted that time, and I felt somehow that we had made this decision together, and we had made the wrong decision. Only I was unchanged, and he was dead. Had I adequately explained the risks of the procedure? I felt I had given him the best care I could, but had some of my anger at him, for destroying his own body, affected my actions? Was I grieving for him less because his death was, in some ways, self-inflicted? Did I grieve for him more because I knew more of him than I did most of my other patients? I realized that I was grieving over my own failure and conflicts as well as his loss, and I grieved for his loss, over the thousands of other deaths that occur every day, because I knew him, I knew something of what he had hoped for, what he had failed at; I knew the music he loved. I knew that on the coast where he lived in Japan, the ocean was a darker blue than anywhere in America, and the waves were very small.

Doctors have been invested with a unique power. With

our knowledge and skill, we can prolong life. If a patient is approved for a liver transplant, sent for the appropriate surgery, or put on the right medication, she will live. She will be granted more life. When the patients do not receive the appropriate treatment, whether deliberately or not, we may cause or hasten their deaths. When we are caring for patients, we cannot judge them; otherwise the power we have been given to prolong life is easily abused. If certain patients are judged unworthy of treatment—for example, if my young patient Nicholas were denied rehabilitation because he is a juvenile delinquent or if Mr. Reynolds were refused surgery because the world doesn't really need another person watching soap operas, or if I were not to receive my life-giving medication because we have too many doctors and writers—then whoever makes these decisions must apply the same standards to himself and to his family. In attempting to define those standards, he will back himself into a corner where he might look around and find himself condemning his own wife or child to death because the numbers don't add up, at which point abstract notions of when and how much to care for a patient always break down. If we start prejudging who is worthy of care and who should be neglected, we enter the dangerous world of eugenics, ethnic cleansing, and racism.

In medicine we are supposed to care for each patient regardless of his or her value—or lack of value—to society: prisoner or preacher, homeless or hero, it is at once an individual and no individual that we care for. It is life we protect, the beating heart, the circuits of the brain, the tiny cells in the bloodstream, the eyes. This is a paradox that is hard to grasp sometimes, as we stand guard over the organs: that we should not judge our patients but that we should know them, that all humans have the same basic bodies and the same basic needs and die and decompose in the same basic ways, but that each life, each complex life that we lose, dies differently, dies differently on the facts of what he hoped for and what he loved and despised and whom he hurt and pleased, disappointed and amazed. My own fragile body is hardly different at all from Mr. Hamilton's, but my life, my life . . .

Human beings are a tangle of emotion and memory, of aspirations and compulsions, of passion and faith. When a human being dies, nothing can replace him. Someone else might do his job, marry his wife, move into his house, but the tangle of thoughts and desires that he was is gone and will never live again. All of us believe that our own lives are priceless, not because of what we might accomplish or what we do for a living but because of what we feel and dream, what we love, what makes us cry, because of who we are. But in order to truly believe in the value of our own lives, we must see the infinite value of the lives of others. If my life is priceless because of what I feel, think, and remember, then the lives of others, including Mr. Hamilton, who also feel, think, and remember must also be priceless. No human being can be replaced; when a man or a woman dies, it is like a species becoming extinct. So much is taken with him. Because I knew Mr. Hamilton, I had a glimpse of just how much was taken with him, and so I grieved. If it were possible to know all the hundreds of thousands of people who die each day, we might grieve for them all.

Since Mr. Hamilton's death, eight more of my patients have died. At some point I know I will lose count, and then I know it might be a challenge to feel for each patient the same loss I felt at the death of one alcoholic veteran, unremarkable to society. But I do hope I never stop feeling a sort of stunned awe and regret when one of my patients leaves this earth, that I at least know enough of that person to know there is a loss. This year I witnessed the deaths of men and women I have known; I have felt their bodies turn cold, and I have wondered, as they ceased to breathe, where the love for the families, the songs they knew by heart, the secrets, where it has all gone, now that the body is no more. It is certainly lost to the living, lost to earth.

BEAUTIFUL FAILURE

For one year of my life, I lived with a lump of scar tissue the size of a grapefruit stuck to the left side of my face. The result of repeated infections of one of my glands, the mass was hard and lumpy. It stretched the overlying skin and the nerves within so that I could not feel the side of my jaw or my lower lip. I was told it would be impossible to remove the scar and that I should learn to live with the deformity. I was twenty-five years old.

In Grand Central Station, a child pointed at me, only to be shushed by her mother. A ticket seller took a step back and asked if I had the mumps. People I hadn't seen in a long time were shocked when they ran into me. They'd heard I'd been ill, and some assumed the lump was a horrible tumor. I did everything I could to shrink it: hot pads, ice packs. I consulted a macrobiotic healer who suggested compresses of barley miso and ginger, which I applied to my face every night. I massaged the spot until the skin was red. Nothing worked. Every time I looked in the mirror, I was reminded of my illness. When I looked at myself, I saw a life alone and an early death.

Tangled within the mass of scar tissue were the remnants of my parotid gland. This gland, the largest salivary gland in the body, sits in front of and around the ear. There are two parotids, one on each side of the face, and they secrete saliva when we eat to help digest the food. Normally the parotid gland is a yellowish pancake of tissue about three inches long, with the texture of a sponge. It is the gland that the mumps virus infects, and before the vaccine, when all children got the mumps, their swollen, miserable faces were a common sight to pediatricians.

The first time I had an infection in my parotid gland, I was twenty-two years old. I had no idea what was causing my face to swell. It was horribly painful to eat; each bite of food caused the infected gland to contract, as if someone were tightening a bolt in my face, tighter and tighter until the bone was about to shatter. I had no idea what was causing this pain. The left side of my face was a little swollen, but I figured it was due to one of my many lymph nodes. I adapted. I wore my hair down to hide the swelling. It hurt to eat, so I didn't eat. When illness first strikes, many people do nothing. Some doctors say this failure to act is denial, but in fact I know as a patient that it is just bewilderment.

I had an appointment with my doctor at Massachusetts General Hospital, so I took the train to Boston. I arrived on Friday night for a Monday appointment. I went to a movie with some friends, a French film, and when my head started pounding halfway through, we attributed it to reading the subtitles. The next night we went out for Chinese food, and I watched the others eat moo shu pork and cashew chicken while I sipped tea.

The morning of my appointment I went to career services at Harvard to begin looking for a job. I had spent the previous year in Egypt on a postgraduate fellowship that I took more for adventure than with any clear career purpose. The doctors who had begun to try to decipher my medical problems had not been happy about this plan. The third world is not considered an ideal vacation spot for people in less-than-perfect health. They had warned me to come home early if I started to feel ill, but since they had not been able to give me a definitive diagnosis, they did not want to proscribe travel altogether. I lasted ten months in Egypt and returned when my jaw started to swell inexplicably. At the time, I was less concerned with my jaw than with the fact that I didn't know what I wanted to do with my life. I had a vague idea about writing but no definite plans. Should I go to graduate school in English literature or try journalism or screenwriting? The people at Harvard career services let me look in their books, though strictly speaking, as a Brown graduate, I was an interloper. I wrote down listings for teachers at inner city schools, for an assistant to a local poet, for an editorial assistant at a publishing company.

By lunchtime my head was throbbing. I took the subway back to the apartment where I was staying and lay down on my friend's futon. My head felt enormous, like a giant pumpkin slammed down on my neck. I couldn't hold it straight, and when I tried to walk, I reeled. I could not lift my head from the pillow without a grand crescendo of pain. It felt as if my skull were filled with sand, and whenever I moved, the sand shifted and knocked against my eyes, dull and heavy. My friend's roommate came home from work and, seeing the state I was in, insisted on accompanying me to the hospital. We took the subway, but I have only a vague memory of the echoes of the station, waiting for the train, a street musician playing a harmonica, and leaning my head against the dirty glass while the lights of each station swelled and crashed, swelled and crashed.

When the doctor at Mass General saw me, he immediately called for a stretcher to take me to the emergency room. I had a temperature of 105 degrees; my heart was racing, 150 beats a minute. Dr. Jacobson helped me onto the stretcher, and I lay down, curled in the fetal position. I could barely move. If I was perfectly still, the pain in my head was steady and rhythmic; I could brace for it. If I shifted, it fell like a blow from a clapper against a bell. Dr. Jacobson told me we needed a spinal tap; he was going to have to put a needle into the space below my spinal cord and withdraw fluid to make sure the infection had not spread to my central nervous system. Later he confided that he had thought this was the beginning of the end for me. Patients with immune deficiencies similar to mine sometimes bumble along for several years before presenting with widespread cancer of the lymph nodes, which essentially destroys the immune system and leads to overwhelming infections and death within a few weeks.

When it was time for the spinal tap, I sat up on the stretcher and hunched my shoulders forward. A nurse stood in front of me so I wouldn't tumble over. Someone swabbed iodine on my back. I stared at the floor. It was a gray putty color with black streaks where the stretchers must have skidded. I barely remember the pain from the needle because the pain in my head was too great.

I've done numerous spinal taps on patients during my training, and it is a measure of my sickness at the time that I have such a poor memory of the one I endured. The needle is ten inches long and about as wide as a coffee stirrer. Gleaming silver, it is hollow on the inside to catch the clear spinal fluid that comes out in drips, at the rate of a slow leak if the pressure is normal. Before the needle plunges in, you numb up the space between the vertebrae in the lower back. The spot you aim for is between the hipbones, which is past where the spinal cord ends. There are only delicate strands of spinal nerves in that area, suspended in the spinal fluid. They are supposed to float away, like scattered fish, from the force of the needle entering, so there is very little risk of nerve damage. I don't remember Dr. Jacobson marking the spot, pressing with his thumbs as I do on patients' backs to feel the depression between the two bones, but as a hematologist, he had probably done hundreds of taps, and since I was young and thin, I was an ideal patient, with clear landmarks and a straight spine.

After the spinal tap, Dr. Jacobson told me I had to be admitted to the hospital. I refused. I had returned to fetal position and was staring at his belt buckle while he talked. His large, soft hands were resting on the guardrail of the stretcher. I couldn't see his face. For some reason, although I could not move, it seemed entirely rational to propose getting on a plane and flying to Atlanta. If I had to be in the hospital, I wanted to go to a hospital at home. He argued that there was no time to fly to Atlanta, but he didn't tell me he thought I was dying. He said I needed antibiotics right away. Somewhere in the middle of this, my parents were called, and my father ordered me to stay at Mass General. My mother told me she would fly up as soon as possible. I was holding the phone next to me on the stretcher, and after they hung up, I didn't want to let it go. The dial tone hummed to me. I held the phone in my arms like a teddy bear, until a nurse came and slipped it away. Then she wheeled me into the emergency room, and I lay weeping behind a curtain.

Some time later someone came to take me to X-ray. I was left in an empty hallway, on my stretcher. There were no patients, no staff; it was absolutely quiet. I waited. I thought maybe I'd been forgotten, although during residency I have seen patients wheeled to vacant waiting rooms hundreds of times. In retrospect, someone was probably just late to get me, but it felt at the time as if I were the only person in the entire building, as if everyone else had fled from some terrible danger and left me there. I overcame my fear of moving to sit up and call for help. No one came. I slipped off the stretcher. The tile floor was cold on my bare feet. My clothes were gone, and I was in a blue hospital gown. A trail of lightbulbs shone down the hall, and I started to follow them. I fell down, then lay on the cold floor. I don't know how long I lay there; it seemed like hours. I called for help, but no one came. The floor was so cold, I thought I might freeze to it. I called out again, a pitiful "Hello!" as if I were just entering a house. Finally a young woman in green scrubs found me. She looked a little disgusted.

"Can you stand?" she asked.

If I had felt better, I would have answered sarcastically, "Yes, I just *wanted* to lie on the floor." Instead I just said no. She disappeared and returned some time later with a large man, who lifted me up to the stretcher as if I were something small and movable, like an apple. They pushed me through a door into an X-ray room. The young woman asked me if I could stand for an X-ray. I said I would try. She positioned me against the wall, my shoulders pushed forward, my chest pressed to the X-ray cartridge, a sort of backward crucifixion. Then she scurried away. I wanted to run with her, but I was still. She shot the film, and I was lifted back onto the stretcher.

Eventually I was sent to a room somewhere in the hospital. Blood was drawn. Antibiotics were started. I had a view of a small corner of the Charles River, which was gray and filmy, like a puddle. I was given something to help me sleep. The next morning my mother arrived.

I had a bacteria growing in my blood, *Streptococcus pneumoniae*. As the name implies, it is the most common bacterial cause of pneumonia, as well as meningitis. It also causes many childhood ear infections. In my case, it had invaded my parotid gland, and there, meeting no resistance, it had multiplied and refortified and then spread into my bloodstream, like an army storming into the roads and rivers of an occupied country. I was lucky. The spinal tap was negative; it had not penetrated into my central nervous system. Streptococcal blood infections can kill in twenty-four hours. One night, when I was an intern in the emergency room, the attending doctor told me that he'd watched a woman exactly my age die from the same infection. In the course of a day, she went from being perfectly healthy to dead.

I, however, was rescued by antibiotics. By the time my mother arrived, I felt better. My head had shrunk to its normal size; the pounding was gone. The infection in my gland had opened up and spilled out into my body, but in doing so, it had released its own poison. After not eating for three days, I was ravenous. I demanded breakfast and wolfed down the flavorless eggs and toast. That afternoon, with my fever broken, my mother took me home. At twenty-two my young body was resilient enough to recover overnight.

But parotitis began to plague me, recurring without warning, shifting from side to side. I would wake up with my face hot and swollen, unable to eat. Since I now knew what this meant, I would start antibiotics right away, and often I was able to stay out of the hospital. When I had to go into the hospital for intravenous antibiotics, they were started before the bacteria could escape from the gland, and I was never septic from parotitis again. Over time, however, the infections consumed the gland, and eventually there was nothing left of it but a scar, a huge scar, a matted weave of fibers and nerves that stubbornly refused to resolve. The gland on the left side of my face simply seized up and turned to stone.

All patients with immune deficiencies are at risk of developing lymphoma, cancer of the immune cells, and there was concern that the lump was more than just a scar. In fact, when I was first evaluated at Mass General, a lymph node was removed that at first appeared to have cancer. Later studies showed that although the lymph node was highly abnormal, it was not cancerous, but given this history, my doctors were concerned that cancer had now developed in the parotid gland. I was referred to an ear-nose-and-throat specialist, or otolaryngologist, at New York Hospital. Dr. Ward stuck a needle into the mass and told me it was benign. There was no evidence of cancer.

He was a kind, thoughtful man, and he carefully considered what to do with me. He showed me a diagram of the parotid gland. At this time, I had never even thought about medical school, and so I was as ignorant of anatomy as I am of planetary cycles. The gland, he explained, lies just beneath the skin and would be easy to remove except for the fact that God has chosen to thread the facial nerve right through its center. This nerve, the seventh cranial nerve, controls all the movements of the face: the smile and the frown, the pucker of the lips, wrinkling of the nose, raising of the eyebrow, all the movements that subtly and unconsciously convey human emotion. If the nerve is cut, the patient is left with a paralyzed face. The edge of her lip will droop down in a permanent frown, and since she cannot close her eyelid, the eye dries out, often resulting in blindness. She can still feel, but her face cannot reveal her emotions. There is no exuberant smile at the sight of her child, no knitted brow of concentration, no wink, no kiss. He ordered an MRI and saw that the scar had wrapped around my facial nerve. The doctor told me that given the size and consistency of my parotid gland, there was no way to remove it without cutting the nerve. Removing it, he said, was purely cosmetic. It was not medically necessary. It was just to make me look better. "Look normal," I remember correcting him.

"A lump," he said, "is better than paralysis."

But I was deformed! I was twenty-five years old. My friends were dating, falling in love, getting married. I could not imagine anyone loving me, with my distorted face. It was an advertisement for my underlying fragility: Who would want to fall in love with a girl who seemed likely to die young? Every time I looked in the mirror, I was reminded of the uncertainty of my future. I stopped looking in the mirror. I didn't allow anyone to take my picture. I hid behind a veil of hair—no ponytails, no barrettes. I avoided parties and preferred the company of dogs to people since, if they noticed my strange face, they didn't say anything. I got used to the stares of grocery store clerks and bank tellers; I got used to people keeping their distance.

I tried to accept the lump on my face. Things could be much worse. It was not a tumor; it was not going to kill me. My deformity was not as pronounced as many. There are patients whose entire faces are scarred from burns. I did not have the congenitally deformed skull of children with birth defects, children with so-called "banana heads" whose skulls closed too early over their brains. I had not lost part of my face to surgery. I did not have the tangle of tumors that afflict patients with Proteus syndrome, like the Elephant Man. If you saw me only from the right, I looked perfectly normal. I hated the lump, but I'd been told to learn to live with it, and so I tried to accept it. I read a lot of books; I hiked alone with my dog. I figured I would never get married. I stepped out of life for a while. Then I met Dr. Gerald Gussack.

My father refused to believe that the mass was inoperable. As a father and a doctor, he could see that condemning a young woman to a lifetime of deformity was, if not a death sentence, then a form of life in prison. Like it or not, our looks define us, and those of us who are distorted, with jagged scars or lost limbs, must first explain these wounds before we introduce ourselves. My father wanted to free me of this burden and asked a colleague for the name of the best head and neck surgeon in Atlanta. He was told to see Gerald Gussack. I was skeptical. A well-respected doctor had already told me that surgery would be foolish. He'd even called in a plastic surgeon to look at me, and they had both agreed: the risk outweighed the benefit. Nonetheless my father insisted on another consultation, and when I went home for Passover that year, he arranged it.

After the seder on Saturday night, I shut the door to my bedroom, the room in which I had grown up, played with model horses, painted a series of pictures of baby animals—the baby wombat still hangs on the wall—learned algebra, written college applications, all those things I did before I was sick. I pulled out the films of the MRI, giant negatives that start at the top of the head and work down through the brain in slices, until they end in a series of white doughnuts that represent the vertebrae. At the level of the eyes, the sockets seem to shoot out like cannonballs, flying in opposite directions. The brain is a jumble of worms. Any metal refracts the image into a starburst, and so my sole tooth filling looked like a small explosion in the back of my mouth. I could not identify the all-important facial nerve, but I traced the outline of the swollen parotid gland—even an untrained eye could see it—and touched my face and imagined myself growing old with it.

On Sunday morning, we drove to Dr. Gussack's office— he had agreed to see us then because I was in town only for the weekend. We arrived a few minutes early. The building was locked, and so we stood, myself and my parents, in front of the sliding glass doors and waited. We did not know whom we were waiting for. My father had only spoken to the doctor on the phone. He could be young or old, short or tall. He could be anyone. Right at ten o'clock, the appointment time, a beige Lexus pulled up. My mother said, "Of course the surgeon drives a Lexus," but instead of a surgeon, a three-year-old boy leaped out. Dressed in miniature surgeon's scrubs and waving an alligator puppet, he ran toward us. He made the alligator puppet roar, and we pretended to be scared, and he laughed, delighted with himself. His father came after him, calling, "Don't scare them, Graham." He extended his hand to my father and said, "Gerald Gussack."

My father shook his hand. Then Dr. Gussack turned to me. He was a handsome man, with bright eyes and a face that seemed to be suppressing a smile, as if he'd just been dancing. He had a wide mustache, like that of an old-fashioned baseball player, and it seemed to make his smile even bigger. "You must be Jamie," he said. He reached out and turned my face gently to one side. He folded the swollen gland in his palm, then traced the outline with his fingertips. "I can get that out," he said. "In fact, I have to." He lifted my chin with his hand. "You're a beautiful girl. We need to give you back your face."

Instantly I fell in love with him.

He opened the building doors, and his son charged inside. We followed him down the empty hallways to his office. Everything was shut up and quiet, the computers off, the chairs tilted up. He had to turn on lights as we went. The little boy ran ahead, flicking light switches and turning on water fountains. Periodically he would rush at us with his puppet, roaring, and we would all scream, to his great pleasure.

The examining room smelled of antiseptic. There was a rigid black vinyl dentist's chair in the center, bolted to the ground. A row of gleaming silver instruments was arrayed on a metal table. A bright lamp hovered overhead, and it occurred to me that in another context the room might be well suited to torture. But I wasn't scared. I'd just been told I was beautiful. I would have settled for just normal looking, but beautiful! There *was* a magic wand, and I had found the man who could wave it.

Dr. Gussack gestured for me to sit down. He took the MRI films from me and hung them up. "It is big," he said. His fingers pressed against the film. "But that doesn't mean I can't do it. It just might take a little longer than usual." He turned to me. "Do you want me to take it out?"

"What about cutting the facial nerve?" He had made no mention of the risk that had deterred the other surgeons.

"That is a risk," he said, "but I've done more difficult operations than this, and all my patients are still smiling." He thought for a moment. "Literally," he added. I didn't understand why he was so confident when the other doctors had been so cautious, but I believed him. I believed his bright eyes and his soft hands and his smile. I believed the man who came to work on a Sunday morning to see me and who brought his yellow-haired boy with him and who told me I was beautiful and promised to take away the mark of my illness.

Looking back, I'm still not sure what separated him from the other surgeons. He may have been cocky, a young surgeon for whom things had always gone right, or he may simply have had more experience with difficult cases. It takes a certain level of confidence just to be a surgeon. When you cut someone open, you are the only one standing between the patient and death. With one slip of the scalpel, you can kill rather than cure. When I watched surgery as a medical student, this truth was chillingly clear. Depending on the surgery, the beating heart or the blood-soaked liver or the arteries to the brain are exposed, those crucial parts of the body that are normally tucked away for protection underneath bone and skin and fat. The surgeon willfully exposes the patient to great danger, in hopes of restoring her to greater health. In a sense, the patient has to be taken down to hell before she can be rescued. In order to take the patient on that journey, the surgeon has to possess a level of confidence that, depending on your perspective and the outcome, can be described as anything from arrogance to poise. I never found Dr. Gussack arrogant, but I also never saw him entertain the possibility that something could go wrong.

In the course of my disease, I have been cared for by numerous doctors. Some I have respected and admired; some I have hated. One I pitied because he seemed so unhappy being a doctor. Some have struggled to understand my disease—they've written to colleagues, they've researched journal articles. Others have shrugged their shoulders and offered me the white flag of a prescription pad. Very few, precious few, have made me feel completely cared for, cupped and cradled, as safe as a three-year-old tucked into bed with the nightlight glowing and the murmur of his parents' voices across the hall. Life is so fraught with peril: airplanes fall from the sky, cars crash, and houses burn. Children get cancer and die; our grandparents succumb to heart attacks and strokes. No one is safe. Religions advise us to thank God for each day, take nothing for granted. Human life does not come with guarantees. And then a doctor comes along and promises to make you well, and if he has some magical combination—a certain look, a certain touch, just the right way of talking—you believe him.

At times I've even felt this power in my own hands, when I sit at a patient's bed and hold his hand and tell him piece by piece the meaning of his lab tests, translating numbers into sentences that in turn translate into life. There are times when I can feel the patient relax under my hands. My father, a cardiologist, once told me that the most important thing he does is lay his fingers on the patient's wrist to feel the pulse. After we leave grade school, the times when we are touched for the sole purpose of reassurance are vanishingly rare. We shake hands and we kiss; we hug briefly at airports, swiftly wrapping and releasing the arms; but we almost never feel the soft stroke of a hand on the forehead or arms rocking us to sleep. No one coos away our nightmares. No one promises to make everything all right and chases the goblins out from under the bed or away from the window. The touch of a doctor is often the closest we come to that reassurance we once cried for nightly, and when Dr. Gussack touched me, I felt it.

Absolute cures are the domain of the surgeon. Internists handle chronic problems, diabetes, high blood pressure, heart failure, immune deficiencies, cirrhosis. Surgeons see a problem, and they cut it out. In medical school, you learn their mantra: a chance to cut is a chance to cure. It is a particularly satisfying field for that reason: there is a beginning and an end. I never expected Dr. Gussack to fix my immune deficiency; he was not going to free me from the constant risk of infection and cancer that my illness poses. He had a clearly defined job: to remove the lump on my face. But in doing that one job, it seemed to me, he would not only give me back my normal face, he would change the tide of the disease. As long as there was permanent damage to my face, it felt as if the disease were winning. If he could make me normal again, we could reclaim the lost ground. I could live a long, normal life, with its ups and downs, its loves and losses.

Three months after I met him, Dr. Gussack took my parotid gland out. He'd warned me to expect a long surgery and a slow recovery: five hours in the operating room and a week in bed. The morning of the surgery, he came into the pre-op area before they put me to sleep. He was wearing a green surgeon's cap and scrubs. His mask was untied, hanging around his neck. I'd already been given an IV, and a wet purple bruise was growing on my forearm where the anesthesia resident had shoved it in. Dr. Gussack noticed it immediately and said, "Who did that to you?" He touched it gently, then laid a hand on my forehead. I was shivering in the thin hospital gown. My hair had been tucked into a blue cap. "Are you ready?" he asked. I nodded.

"You'll be fine, sweetheart," he said.

A nurse asked him if it was okay to start sedating me, and he nodded. She injected some medicine, and I drifted off, with his hand still on my head.

I woke up in the recovery room, four hours of my life snipped out. I vomited, registered that I was alive, and fell back asleep. Then I woke up in a room on the eighth floor of the hospital. My mother was sitting next to my bed reading a magazine. The television was on but muted. She didn't notice I was awake until I said, "Hi." My mouth was dry and cracked. Out of the corner of my eye, on the pillow next to me, I could see a plastic bulb, the end of a drain sewn into my neck to remove any blood that might ooze out after the surgery. She called to my father that I was awake.

"Everything went great," they told me. "The doctor said it was easy."

When Dr. Gussack came by later that afternoon, he said he'd done two other operations after mine. "Yours was the tricky one," he said. He winked at me. He traced the outline of my ear and told me, "I buried your stitches behind here. No one will ever see your scar, unless you show it to them." He touched me gently along the bandage. "I even buried the stitches from the biopsy they did in New York. You're going to be beautiful again."

I glanced at myself in the mirror. My head was wrapped in a white bandage, like a soldier's in the Civil War. My face was bruised and swollen. I didn't look too beautiful right at that moment. Dr. Gussack read my mind. He said, "Well, you have to give it a few days."

He had done the surgery in less than two hours. The gland had been swollen to the size of a fist and had the texture of rope. He wanted to remove it quickly, to avoid depriving the nerve of oxygen, and he'd been pleased with his own speed. Before he left the room, he told me to pucker my lips and smile. I did both, albeit weakly, and he nodded to himself. I could see he was pleased, so pleased it seemed that for a moment he didn't want to share it, even with me. This was his accomplishment, and I was just the beneficiary.

My father thanked him profusely. "Please," Dr. Gussack said. "I was just doing my job."

The next morning he unwrapped the bandages. I was still swollen, but I recognized my face in a way I had not for the past nine months. It was the face I'd known and watched evolve for twenty-six years, the face that defined me. I felt like myself again. I was not in any pain at all, just a little groggy from the anesthesia. The drain was still hanging from my neck, but my father assured Dr. Gussack that he could take care of it. I went home.

I recovered remarkably quickly from the operation, more quickly than I had when my tonsils were taken out at age nineteen. My mother had stocked the house with ice cream and pudding, but I was able to eat everything from egg rolls to pizza. If I held a compact mirror up to the mirror in the bathroom and leaned my head forward, I could see the stitches, a train track of them curved behind my ear. Two days after I went home, I had the drain removed. That night I went to a play. The next day I returned to my apartment, where I had been working on my essay for medical school applications.

I saw Dr. Gussack a week after the surgery. He removed the stitches and ran his fingers along the line of the incision. "How do you feel?" he asked.

I told him I felt great. "It's good to look normal again."

"Better than normal," he said.

I smiled. He stared at my smile. "Do that again," he said.

The smile was a little crooked. He asked me to pucker my lips, which I could do normally, but I could not blow up my left cheek. One of the tiny branches of the facial nerve had been damaged, causing these deficits. "It will probably get better," he reassured me.

I told him that a crooked smile was better than a lump on the face.

"Maybe," he said, "but I aim for perfection."

Three days after I saw him, Dr. Gussack called my father with grave news. He told him that the pathology report showed cancer of the lymph nodes. It seemed to him that I was going to need chemotherapy. He was unaware that five years before, when I was first evaluated at Massachusetts General Hospital, they had found similar pathology, only to learn that there was no cancer.

I've often wondered why Dr. Gussack called my father rather than me. I was twenty-six years old when I had the surgery, an adult, and legally he was obligated to tell me first. But just as he made me feel as safe as a child, I think he still saw me as a child, and he wanted to protect me from this devastating information. My father is a doctor, so doctor to doctor he might have been able to retreat into the language of medicine, using words like *staging* and *prognosis* rather than having to discuss the horror of chemotherapy, hair loss, sterility, the possibility of death. Head and neck surgeons often diagnose cancer, but almost always it is in older patients, the product of years of smoking and drinking. It is more difficult to give a deadly diagnosis to a patient you perceive as innocent, a child or a young woman. When disease is random, it is unsettling. When it strikes the young, it reminds us all of our vulnerability.

Years later in an ethics class, I mentioned this indiscretion on the part of Dr. Gussack. (I didn't use his name.) The doctor running the discussion said that what he had done was unconscionable. I think it was, if anything, conscionable, and I imagine it had more to do with empathy than ethics. In addition to the little boy I met, Dr. Gussack had a ten-year-old daughter. He might have seen a possible fate for her in what had befallen me. Like me, she would play on a soccer team, take art classes, study Africa in social studies. She would graduate from high school, go on to college. And then suddenly, mysteriously, she would fall ill. He probably felt that he would not want his daughter to hear such news all alone in a doctor's office, and so for this and who knows how many other reasons—to respect my family, to avoid his own sorrow—he called my father. I never asked him, and now it is too late.

After my surgery, I saw Dr. Gussack infrequently, but I still felt close to him. Every time I looked in the mirror, I was reminded of what he had done for me. When I did see him, he always asked about the other parotid gland. It, too, had been infected numerous times, and he wanted to operate on it before the gland became as scarred as the one he'd removed. But after each infection it had always shrunk to close-to-normal size, and it wasn't bothering me. I was being treated for my immune deficiency, and I was confident that I was not going to get any more parotid infections anyway. And there was still some minor residual nerve damage from the first operation. I decided to wait. If worse came to worst,

I reasoned, he could handle any difficulty a subsequent infection might present.

During my first year of medical school, Dr. Gussack delivered one of our anatomy lectures. That afternoon he showed up in the anatomy lab to help with the head and neck dissections. In the grim room, cadavers in various stages of dissection lay on cold metal tables, reeking of formaldehyde. Muscles, dissected away from bone, swung stiffly with each movement of the body, and all the individual pieces that make up a human being hung by threads: the eyes, the tendons, the tongue, all freed from their confines. My anatomy partners and I had already dissected the brain, and we had sawed off the top of the skull, which lifted open like a jewelry box. We had named our cadaver Grammy Hall, after the Jew-hating grandmother who glares at Woody Allen in *Annie Hall*, since she was an old woman, almost certainly someone's grandmother, and we reasoned that she disliked us—why else did her muscles and tendons and nerves hide whenever we sought them out? It seemed we inevitably found whatever nerve or artery we were looking for right after we had cut it. We kept ourselves amused during the late hours by imagining the deficits Grammy would be experiencing at our hands were she alive. Oops, there goes the chorda tympani—she can't taste anything. Uh-oh, we severed the ophthalmic artery—now we've blinded her. Shoot! We've cut the radial nerve; her hand is paralyzed. Our hilarity was tempered by an undercurrent of fear: one day live bodies would rest below our hands.

When Dr. Gussack saw me, he greeted me as he always did: "Hi, sweetheart." Then he asked, "Have you seen it?"

"Seen what?"

"The parotid."

He sat down at one of the cadaver tables, picked up a

scalpel, and in one steady move sliced from the top of the ear to the neck. I compared his incision to our incisions: it was perfectly smooth and exactly the right depth. He had known just where to cut to avoid every major structure. With a single snip, he freed the skin of the face and peeled it away to reveal a tangle of nerves and vessels, all intact. He gingerly lifted a vessel aside and pointed. "There it is." He showed me a yellow-white mass of tissue, lumpy and the texture of wet wool. "Yours was much bigger," he said, "and tougher." He examined the gland. Then, noting something that was completely invisible to me, he said, "Look." He took a forceps and extracted from the jumble a shiny white strand, not much thicker than dental floss. "That's the nerve." He pointed with the scalpel. "Five branches. Temporal. Zygomatic. Buccal. Mandibular. Cervical." He looked at me. "Smile," he said. I obliged, and he looked genuinely distressed. My smile was still crooked.

He sighed, then asked me, "Which branch is damaged?"

"The mandibular."

"Which branch of the mandibular?"

"The marginal."

"To what muscle?"

"The orbicularis oris."

He shook his head. "Well, you won't forget that, will you, sweetheart?"

I was pleased that I had known the answers to his questions, but it saddened me to see how upset he was, as if this one tiny mistake could in any way diminish what he had done for me. "I like having a crooked smile," I said. "It gives me character. Humphrey Bogart had a crooked smile."

"I'm glad you don't mind, sweetheart," he said, "but I aim for perfection."

He touched the right side of my face, where my remaining parotid gland sat, always a little swollen. "I won't make any mistakes when I take this one out. I promise."

I saw Dr. Gussack again a few months later when I was scheduled to have a lymph node removed. I needed tubes in my ears and a bone marrow biopsy, and I decided to have all these painful procedures done while I was sedated for the lymph node biopsy. Dr. Gussack and Dr. Tom Heffner, the hematologist, and Dr. Ira Horowitz, the gynecologist, all came in succession and placed my tubes and withdrew bone marrow and cut out the lymph node. I'd had each of these procedures numerous times before, and I was not having general anesthesia, so I had convinced my parents to stay home and arranged for my boyfriend to pick me up. Still, some impulse compelled Dr. Gussack to call my father after the procedure, just to say that I was fine.

I finished the first year of medical school and started the second. I acquired a stethoscope and a white coat, and I began learning the art of physical diagnosis, of looking at ears and eyes and listening to hearts and lungs. Once a week the second-year medical students went to the hospital and tried to learn how to be doctors, how to talk to and touch a patient. I was painfully shy. I felt like an impostor in my white coat, and I was reluctant to ask patients to lift their shirts to allow me to listen to their heartbeats, knowing full well I could not interpret the vague, distant sounds I heard.

One day, when I was about to leave for the hospital, my father called and told me to go and see Dr. Gussack. I told him I was hearing and feeling fine, but he corrected me. Dr. Gussack, he told me, had been diagnosed with a brain tumor. He was now a patient in the hospital where he was usually a physician, the hospital where I was training and where I had had my surgery.

I learned later that Dr. Gussack had had a seizure. Knowing that a seizure is an ominous sign in an otherwise healthy person, he had ordered a CT scan. I heard that he read the scan himself, though now, as a doctor, I doubt this is true. A radiologist would have seen it first. Still, as with all legends, it heightens the story: the heartbreaking image of this young man, a husband, a father of two, a doctor, standing alone in a dark room, eerily lit with the gray films of skulls and bones, examining the picture that for him foretold the future more surely than any crystal ball. In the front of his brain was a large tumor, the size of a ragged plum. He would have recognized it immediately; it was a death sentence. The scan showed a type of brain tumor called a glioblastoma multiforme. On the film, it would have shown up as an evil white blob, visible even to the untrained eye, with tentacles choking the deepest recesses of the brain, where memory and love are stored.

The glioblastoma is fairly rare—there are only about twelve hundred cases a year—but the tumor is uniformly fatal and unresponsive to treatment; eighty percent of those it strikes die within a year, and by the time of death, most have lost a significant portion of brain function. They die as remnants of the men and women that they were, their memories and movements lost to both the cancer and the surgeries that are performed to try to fight it.

Dr. Gussack would have known all of this as he looked at the black-and-white picture of his brain. He would also have known how much of cancer in general, and of this tumor in particular, remains a mystery. He would know that the glioblastoma in his brain is one of the great killers of biology, an atomic bomb of cancer cells that does not so much grow as explode. Because of the education and training he had received, he would know that the tumor would kill him, sooner rather than later, in months rather than years. But he would not know—nor could he ever know—why it had happened to him. He would not know if the same fate would befall his children, and of course he would not know what—if anything—awaited him after the cancer had destroyed his body.

When I saw Dr. Gussack, his head had been shaved. He'd had surgery two days before to debulk the tumor. It is all but impossible to entirely remove a glioblastoma. Surgery is done to prevent the massive tumor from squeezing the brain; it buys months, not years. A train track of staples ran from the base of his neck over the top of his head to his eyebrow. He had received medication to bring down the swelling in his brain, and the medicine had caused his face to fill with water, so that with his newly bald head and his round cheeks, he looked at once very young and very old—the round sweet face of a baby with the sad and fearful eyes of a man approaching death, an old man.

I held out the flowers I had brought, some generic yellow chrysanthemums and pink carnations. The room was full of flowers. He gestured for me to put them down, and then he said, "Hi, sweetheart," as he always did, as if I were sitting in the examining room and he were caring for me.

I said, "My father called and told me you were in the hospital." Neither of us acknowledged why. "I'm so sorry," I said.

He didn't say anything, and after a moment I noticed that his eyes were not focused on mine but rather to the right and down, to where my remaining parotid gland sat, always slightly swollen.

"Are you looking at my parotid gland?" I asked him.

"We should have taken it out when we had a chance."

"I can wait until you get better," I said, and immediately felt like an idiot. We both knew he was not getting better. Even if he somehow survived his tumor, with a large portion of his frontal lobe removed, he would never operate again.

He beckoned me closer to the bed. He was wearing an Atlanta Braves T-shirt, shorts, and slippers, an outfit in which one rarely sees one's doctor. But he still felt like my doctor. He bent my head down and circled my left ear with his hand, pulling it forward to examine the scar he'd left behind. It was all but invisible, no wider than a thread, but his eye could find it, the surgeon's signature, the mark that he had forever changed another human being.

I told him, "No one knows it's there unless I show it to them."

He smiled. "Then it is our secret."

If this scene were to happen now, I think I would behave differently. Since that day, I have numerous times been in the room when a patient is told he is dying. More than once I have been the one telling him, and I have learned that failing to acknowledge death just leaves the patient alone in his despair. I would like to have told Dr. Gussack that although I knew I could do nothing to change the course of his disease, at least I recognized its basic injustice; at least I could be angry and sad for him, with him. It is a natural and necessary impulse to deny death; every day we are confronted with its possibility, and in order to get on with life, we have to ignore our own vulnerability. This response is reasonable until you reach the point where death is imminent. Then pretending that life is endless becomes cruel, and the patient who knows he is dying finds himself screaming the truth against a sea of nay-sayers. I wish that I could have made

Dr. Gussack feel less alone by simply acknowledging the tragedy of what was happening to him instead of standing there blindly and insisting that nothing had changed when, in fact, for him everything had changed.

I saw Dr. Gussack only one more time before he died. I had offered to baby-sit for his children or to help out in any way that he and his wife needed, but in the end he was a much greater part of my life than I was of his, which is true for most patients and most doctors. The doctor has many patients, but the patient only one doctor, or a few. I actually knew very little of him. I didn't know what made him laugh, what movies he liked, where he went on vacation. I didn't know if he was happily married, if he was close to his parents, if he was religious or agnostic. And yet his death left an enormous space in my life, a space that had been filled by something much bigger than one man. It had been filled by a hero.

Dr. Gussack had friends and family to help him, and he had his own set of doctors caring for him. I hoped that some of them could make him feel as safe and as calm as he had made me feel, though in the end he would know that none could save him. One of the sacrifices you make as a doctor is that, knowing the limits of medicine, you lose some hope. Patients who are ignorant of medicine have the option of clinging to miracles. During my internship, I cared for a young woman named Lisa who had relapsed from leukemia. I was particularly struck by her because her birthday was just two days before mine. Lisa had failed all treatment, and she was kept alive with blood and platelet transfusions. The cancer had filled her bones and blood vessels and brain, and she was told, repeatedly, that she had days or weeks to live. She was on a morphine drip, and she would walk the corridor, pushing her IV pole with morphine and dark red blood flowing into her veins. Despite everything her doctors told her, despite her harrowed face and her tremendous pain, she told me, "I can't be dying. All the women in my family live to be a hundred." At first I thought she was putting on a brave face, but later I saw she believed she was going to live. She was making Christmas lists; she imagined names for the child she would have when she got better. She thought maybe she'd finish college. Two weeks later she died.

Physicians do not allow themselves such illusions. Wild hopes break down in the face of knowledge, and though other terminal patients hold out until the end for a miracle cure, disbelieving their doctors and searching for answers on the Internet, Dr. Gussack would not have allowed himself such myth-making. I know this now that I am a doctor. My husband and my mother still persist in the belief that there is an answer for the ambiguities in my life: Why is that gland swollen? What are the long-term effects of these medicines? Why is your eye red? In the course of becoming a doctor, I have learned the explanation for some of the manifestations of my illness, but for every answered question there are ten unanswered, and becoming a doctor includes learning not only what we know but how much we don't know. Before I was a doctor, I sometimes hoped for a miracle cure; the best I hope for now is to continue in my current state of health for the rest of my life, not cured but stable.

I saw Dr. Gussack for the last time more than a year after his diagnosis. He had outlived his allotted six months, though I had heard that he had been through another surgery to debulk the rapidly growing tumor and had received more radiation therapy. The cost of each day was getting higher.

I was not expecting to see him. We were not in the hospital and not at the clinic. My father and I were attending a fund-raiser for organ transplantation in a fancy restaurant. For a ridiculous price, you could spend an evening playing Ping-Pong, darts, air hockey, and blackjack with players for the Braves or Falcons in a restaurant designed to look like an antebellum mansion with a circular driveway leading up to a white-columned front porch. I arrived in my Corolla and waited for valet parking behind a line of Mercedes-Benzes and BMWs.

This is not the kind of event I would normally attend, since I'm not much of a sports fan and can't afford the contributions necessary to move in such circles, but I had been given the tickets, and I thought my father would enjoy it. The restaurant was crowded with doctors from the community as well as businessmen, wives, girlfriends. Loud music was playing, and people were swimming in drinks and posing for pictures with the baseball and football players, strapping young men with bulging biceps and mouths full of white teeth.

I didn't recognize any of them, but my father pointed out the famous ones, often along with batting averages, touchdowns scored, positions played. They all looked the same to me, and I couldn't get excited about meeting them, but I was clearly alone in my ennui. Others rushed over to them, waving fifty-dollar bills for a chance to compete in air hockey or foosball. I looked around. A disc jockey was taking requests. Up on a makeshift stage, two young women with waxy red lips were kissing the cheeks of a blond-haired baseball player. Across the room, I saw Dr. Gussack.

He was utterly changed, shrunken and hollowed out. His eyes had fallen back into his head as if he were collapsing inward, and he had the pale, bloodless face of a patient on chemotherapy. He was bald, except for a few wiry strands of colorless hair, and he had lost his handlebar mustache. All around me were the supposed modern-day heroes: these massive men who win adoration and millions of dollars just for playing a game, while across the room was my hero, the shadow of a man on a folding chair.

Dr. Gussack saw me, too. He smiled. I edged through the crowd to where he was sitting with his wife. What she must have been through those last twelve months!

"Hi, sweetheart," he said. I could barely hear him over the noise.

The medicine was keeping his face puffy and fat, so that it appeared as if he were being replaced by some other substance from the inside out. Whatever had made up his body and his mind before had been removed—surgically, and with the poison of radiation and drugs—and only the shell of him was left, with stuffing where the blood and bones used to be.

I don't really remember what I said to him; what I remember was trying not to cry.

As always, Dr. Gussack bent my head forward to see my scar. Sick as he was, his touch still comforted me. "Even I can barely see it," he said. I felt his fingers trace the line where the deformity had been.

"It's our secret," I said. I don't think he remembered saying that to me. The brain surgeries had probably taken some of his memories. In any event, he was always larger in my life than I in his, the words he spoke to me more memorable, I am sure, than my answers.

My father saw us talking and came over. He shook Dr.

Gussack's hand and told him, as always, "We're so grateful for what you did for Jamie."

"I was just doing my job," he said.

We all stared at each other for a minute. In retrospect, perhaps I should have hugged him. Perhaps I should have acknowledged the injustice of what was happening to him. I should have said good-bye in a way that would let him know how much I would mourn him. I should have thanked him again for saving my life. I should have grabbed his legs and begged him not to die. I looked at his wife, a lovely woman with long, straight hair. She looked exhausted, and I wondered what it must be to count not each day but each minute.

Then we said good-bye. We said good-bye as if we were going to see him tomorrow or the next time there was fundraiser for kidney transplants and we wanted to play Ping-Pong with a football star. He melted into the crowd. My father and I turned around. We decided to leave soon after that.

It is always awful to see the humbling of a hero—the athlete who competes past his prime and stumbles, the artist whose late paintings show only madness, the saint who transgresses—but most of us see our heroes only from afar. We read about them in books; we watch them on TV. We ask them for autographs at events like the one we were attending that night where they stay on their pedestals, and we stay far below them.

Dr. Gussack wasn't a huge man; he wasn't paid millions of dollars, and no one would have worn a certain brand of shoes or drunk a certain soft drink just because he did. But he was my hero more surely than any athlete or movie star, and he had touched me, exposed the blood and bone of my body and healed me. He had saved me in a way that to me was nothing short of miraculous, only to be pushed to his knees by disease, by exactly that which the physician dedicates his life to opposing. But of course we always lose. Death always wins eventually, and I, still a medical student when I saw Dr. Gussack that night, knew that I had chosen a profession doomed to a beautiful, honorable failure.

Dr. Gussack died three months after I saw him at the fundraiser. There was a memorial service for him at the synagogue, and I went, with my parents and, to my amazement, hundreds of other people—his colleagues, his friends, his patients. Dr. Gussack's family sat stoically while the testaments were read. I had always felt as if I were his favorite patient, but as others spoke, I realized that he made all his patients feel that way. That did not diminish my affection for him. I sat in awe of a man who could touch so many.

Finally at the very end of the service, after everyone else had spoken, a boy rose from his chair and approached the stand. The rabbi had to bend the microphone down to reach him. It was Dr. Gussack's son, now eight years old He was wearing a suit and tie, dressed up to look like a little man. He squeezed the microphone, and without crying, he declared, "If you think you know how much I loved my dad, then you don't know how much I loved my dad."

My loss was nothing compared to his, but I grieved nonetheless. A man who had given me something great was gone, and I would never be able to repay him. Dr. Gussack gave me back my face; he made me look normal again, which is no small thing. Ask anyone who does not look normal. Without his help, I am convinced, I would have crept deeper into the shell of my disease. I would have always considered myself ill, not a participant, someone just waiting to die. His death shook me because it left me more alone in my illness, and I wondered how alone he had felt in his. I would have liked to have told him that, while he was here, he did more than diagnose and operate. He broke a hole in the wall that illness erects around each patient, and for a while at least, he brought light into the lonely prison of my disease.

ALL TOO HUMAN

A patient came into the clinic last month complaining that his hand still hurt from minor surgery that had been done three months ago. On examination my colleague found a shiny black thread sticking up through the jagged scar left by his stitches. The surrounding skin was red and peeling. With forceps he pulled out the thread. It was a piece of suture material. The surgeon had placed permanent stitches inside the patient's hand when he should have used dissolvable stitches. Unable to absorb the stitch, the body had kept fighting, which led to chronic inflammation and pain in the affected hand. In order to remove the stitch, we had to numb the patient's hand, cut it open, pull out the stitches, and put in the correct sutures. The lesion healed well, and when he returned ten days later to have the new stitches removed, there was no sign of the previous trauma.

During internship I was once called in the middle of the night by a nurse who noted that on the last shift a patient had been given an antibiotic called clindamycin when one called ciprofloxacin had been ordered. The patient appeared fine. When I went to see him, he was watching television and reading a magazine, in Greek, he told me. He did not have a fever; his heart rate was normal, and his lungs were clear. He was being treated for an infection in his foot. Clindamycin and ciprofloxacin are similar drugs, though each kills a specific set of bacteria better than the other. Since the patient's infection was localized, missing one dose of his scheduled antibiotic was not likely to have serious consequences. I noted the error in an incident report and told the nurse to give him the right medication at his next scheduled dose.

A friend from medical school called a few months ago to tell me that he might have hastened the demise of one of his patients in the coronary care unit. The patient, an elderly man, had been admitted for a massive heart attack. He had been stabilized, but his damaged heart was racing along at twice the normal rate, putting him at risk for further tissue damage. Previous attempts to slow his heart had produced a more dangerous situation, called heart block, in which the signal for the heart to beat is not transmitted. My friend decided to try once more, very carefully, with a very low dose of medication. The medicine slowed the patient's heart, but then he went into heart block again, and finally his heart stopped beating altogether. My friend was able to resuscitate him, but not before the patient suffered severe brain injury from lack of oxygen. The patient's chances of surviving his massive heart attack were poor to begin with, and now that he was on a respirator and unlikely to regain enough brain function to breathe on his own, his prognosis was terrible.

I once cared for a sixty-one-year-old woman with severe congestive heart failure. Her heart was stretched thin as paper and was so weak that it could barely pump; her blood leaked out in trickles instead of waves. She could not maintain a high enough blood pressure to walk. Whenever she stood up, she got light-headed and fell. There was no way to reverse the damage to her heart. She sat in the hospital for weeks while I tried every combination of drugs to increase her blood pressure without overflowing her lungs. Nothing worked. Finally, after a discussion with the patient and her daughter, we decided to send her to physical therapy, where she would learn to use a walker or a wheelchair. She was discharged from the hospital but returned three days later in septic shock. She had a urinary tract infection that had spread to her bloodstream. It was possible that she had developed the infection while she was in the hospital, but I had not examined her urine in a week. I had been focused on her heart. She was readmitted to the hospital and started on three different antibiotics, but with her failing heart she could not withstand sepsis, and after seven days in the intensive care unit, she died of multisystem organ failure.

When I was a medical student, a baby named only Baby Boy Greene was helicoptered in from a small town two hours south of Atlanta, barely alive. The obstetrician who had delivered the baby had underestimated his size at nine pounds; he turned out to be a massive twelve. The doctor had recommended a cesarean section, but the mother had wanted to deliver vaginally, and the doctor had not insisted. Had he known the baby was twelve pounds, he would not have given her a choice. In modern obstetrics, twelve-pound babies are always delivered by C-section; the risk to mother and baby is too great. During the delivery, the baby's head had jammed in the mother's pelvis. The umbilical cord was squeezed, depriving the baby of oxygen. The baby was finally pulled through with forceps, but he suffered head trauma and oxygen deprivation. The baby was left brain-damaged, and his mother bled to death.

Every few months, it seems, egregious medical errors make headlines: the wrong side of the brain operated on, the wrong limb amputated, a boy's penis cut off during a routine circumcision, a woman given a fatal dose of medication. Recently *The New York Times* reported seventy thousand deaths due to medical errors in Veterans Administration hospitals. The February 2000 issue of *Harper's* magazine states that the number of deaths by medical mistakes in 1998 equaled the number of deaths in automobile accidents. I'm not sure how they arrived at these numbers. Medical errors occur, but they are rarely as clear-cut as the cases that make headlines.

The patient with the wrong kind of stitches was inconvenienced and experienced three months of unnecessary discomfort. He was the victim of a plain and simple error, but the damage could be repaired equally simply. Giving the patient the wrong antibiotic was a clear mistake, but again, the consequences were limited. On the other hand, the obstetrician who misjudged the size of the baby made a grievous error with terrible consequences.

My failure to do a simple urinalysis on my patient in heart failure may have resulted in her death. I have thought and rethought the case. A more experienced doctor might have considered that her continued low blood pressure—despite full medical intervention—could be due to an infection, even though her urine, blood, and sputum had been checked for possible infection at her admission. She had never mounted a fever, but sick, elderly people—I now know—often do not become febrile. In the chain of command in a teaching hospital, I was not ultimately responsible. I was an intern, overseen by a resident and an attending physician, but we had thirty patients on our hospital service, an overwhelming number, and my patient's infection went unsuspected until it was too late.

My friend's case in the coronary care unit was ultimately a judgment call that went the wrong way. The medication he gave is routinely used to slow heart rate. The patient's racing heart was endangering his health, and he was at high risk for another heart attack if it could not be controlled. My friend gave a quarter of the regular dose and watched cautiously as the drug was infused. He did nothing wrong, but the outcome was terrible. Given the patient's poor response to the medicine in the past, some doctors might view his decision as an error, others as bad luck. Every doctor, at some point in his career, will make a decision with poor, even fatal, consequences. He will probably make more than one such decision. It's the price you pay for working in the medium of human life. And although on paper this margin of error seems inevitable and therefore grimly acceptable, it is wholly unjust and unforgivable to the patient who is its victim.

A clear-cut mistake may have no consequences at all, while a reasonable judgment call—a case in which there is no simple, correct answer and the physician must consult what she knows as fact and her own experience to make an educated guess—may result in disaster or a miraculous cure. Most patients don't want to accept that in medicine, despite our vast knowledge, a great deal is still left to chance. Most of that chance is simply due to the fact that what we know in medicine is dwarfed by what we have yet to discover, but beyond that mountain of guessing lie the smaller whims of human frailty and error. Everything from the personality of the doctor to the medications available at a certain hospital can influence a patient's outcome, but most of us prefer to think of medicine as a tightly tuned machine, a player piano with a limited repertoire that it reproduces identically, year after year. This assumption keeps us from being crippled by fear each time we enter a hospital, in the same way that we assume each time we board a plane that a series of ordered events will follow. When this assumption is shattered—as it was in September 2001—we are shaken. And we are quick to cover up this glimpse of human fallibility with more computers, more print-outs, more inspections, and more controls.

In order to minimize mistakes, medicine is an increasingly regimented system with built-in redundancies and checks and balances. In our hospital, for example, when a doctor orders a medicine, the pharmacy staff checks to see if the standard dosage has been requested. If not, the pharmacist will tell the doctor to recheck the order. The pharmacist has a list of the patients' drug allergies and is also responsible for notifying the physician if two drugs that are known to have adverse interaction have been ordered. The nurses check the drugs the pharmacy sends to the patient's room against the doctor's orders. If blood products are given, two nurses must confirm that the type and amount match the patient and the doctor's orders.

Most diagnoses also follow regimented steps. There are rigid algorithms for managing disease that every medical student and resident must learn: acute pancreatitis, diabetic ketoacidosis, renal failure, septic shock, third-degree burns, appendicitis—all these conditions and hundreds more have step-by-step plans for workup, diagnosis, and treatment. Every intern carries a book in the pocket of her white coat that summarizes these steps: which blood tests and X-rays to order, which drugs and fluids to administer, which specialists to consult. During internship I carried a plastic card in my pocket outlining the steps of running a code if a patient's heart stops. In another pocket was a green book called *Facts and Formulas*, a cheat sheet for calculating lung, heart, and kidney function. Stuffed behind that was *The Washington Manual*, the intern's bible, with outlines for managing almost any problem in internal medicine.

Given all this information, it seems odd that medical errors happen at all, but despite the algorithms and the checks and balances, they do. They happen because patients almost never present with a "classic" form of a given disease. They rarely have only one disease, and they never wave their hands as they roll by on the stretcher, point at their chests, and call out, "Right lower lobe pneumonia!" More often the signs and symptoms are suggestive of more than one disease. A cough and fever usually mean pneumonia, but they could also be cancer. Add in weight loss, and you think cancer, but people lose weight with emphysema and heart failure and AIDS as well. The body tricks you. Nerves start in one place and end in another, so that abdominal pain can actually reflect inflammation in the lungs; back pain can mean pancreatitis. When I had pancreatitis, it hurt to breathe, and the first diagnosis, quite rationally, was probable pleurisy. Diabetics urinate frequently, but so do men with enlarged prostates. Patients who complain of fatigue can have anything from leukemia to depression. Chest pain can come from the heart, the chest muscles, the ribs, or the lungs.

We order tests to further define the diagnosis and meanwhile treat in whatever way we think appropriate. If the chest pain is accompanied by changes on the electrocardiogram, heparin, a blood thinner, is almost always given to minimize heart damage in case of a heart attack. If, however, the chest pain is the result of anemia—low blood counts causing the heart to work harder, since there's less blood to carry oxygen—and the anemia is the result of internal bleeding, the blood thinner could kill the patient. Physicians almost never make a decision with certainty. Instead, we make decisions, order tests and medications, and even operate on the basis of probability: likely, possible, or rare.

We often say that medicine is an art, not a science. In a science all the variables must be defined. A hypothesis is formulated, and an experiment is conducted to prove or disprove it. Controls are set up to provide a yardstick against which results are measured. A positive control is guaranteed to have the expected outcome; a negative control is guaranteed not to. All the steps in the experiment are recorded until results are obtained. The process is repeated and repeated to make sure that under these well-defined circumstances the same thing always happens: a cell makes a certain protein, a molecule shatters into atomic particles, a laboratory mouse dies. But such rigid consistency is not possible in medicine. The best we can do is to take the science that has been proven in the laboratory and apply it, case by case, to each patient. There are no positive and negative controls. There is no way to define every variable. We do our best to assess the function of the heart and the liver, the blood and the kidneys, but since there is still so much we do not know of the human body, we are left guessing. *Art* is another word for the delicate guessing that we do.

Most poor outcomes in medicine are inevitable: the patient has a fatal disease. Aside from that, death and disability usually result from judgment calls that go the wrong way: a patient is given life-saving chemotherapy but dies from the treatment. Occasionally there are outright mistakes—a lab misinterpreted, the wrong medicine given. Least frequent of all, but sadly real, are the mistakes that result from arrogance, incompetence, and malice. When I was hospitalized in the spring of 1999, I experienced each kind of mistake for myself.

To examine the errors—and also to appreciate how difficult it is to manage the course of an illness—I will summarize the events of the illness, essentially as they would appear in a discharge summary. The discharge summary must include those facts that future physicians might need to know in managing the patient: antibiotics used, procedures done, results of radiologic studies. It is also a legal document, and any appropriate interventions and monitoring must be recorded in the event of future litigation. Beyond that the details of the story—those details that fiction writers and playwrights are told to include to make a character and a time and a place seem real—are omitted. The fact that a consultation was not done until one day after it was requested, for example, or that a lab value was not drawn, would not be included. Most of the time these details have no impact, and they are not mentioned any more than what meal the President ate on the plane on his way to Bosnia would be included in a newspaper article. They are tangential to the story. The story in the discharge summary takes place in any time and any place, and the patient is referred to as "the patient," a male or female of a certain age and a certain race upon whose body certain events took place.

Chief Complaint: "I have parotitis."

History of Present Illness: The patient is a 33-year-old white female with an undefined congenital immune deficiency. Three weeks prior to admission, the patient noted cough, nasal congestion, and lymph node swelling associated with an upper respiratory tract infection. She was given cough syrup and prednisone, 20 mg a day, but developed swelling in her parotid gland and was admitted to the hospital with the diagnosis of acute parotitis, which the patient noted has occurred several times in the past. She received two days of intravenous Timentin and Solu-Medrol and was discharged on oral antibiotics and prednisone. The patient improved for a short time, but the swelling recurred and the patient was readmitted.

Past Medical and Surgical History: Status post left parotidectomy 1993, status post tonsillectomy and adenoidectomy 1986, repeat adenoidectomy 1988, status post cone biopsy 1995, status post LEEP 1996, 1997, status post lymph node biopsy 1987, 1988, 1992, 1994, 1995, status post bone marrow biopsy 1987, 1988, 1990, 1991, 1992,

1993, 1994, 1995, 1996. History of herpes esophagitis 1991, history of herpes zoster (shingles) 1980, history of parotitis, 1988 × 2, 1989 × 3, 1990 × 2, 1991, history of pancreatitis 1989, history of pneumococcal sepsis 1988, Sicca syndrome.

Medications: Vancomycin 1 g IV q day, alpha interferon 3 million units subcutaneous every other day, intravenous gammaglobulin 20 grams q month, prednisone 20 mg q day

Review of Systems: Significant for facial pain. Denies fever, chills, night sweats, weight loss, cough, difficulty breathing, chest pain, nausea, vomiting, diarrhea.

Physical Exam:

Blood pressure: 121/68; *Heart rate:* 92; *Respiratory rate:* 16; *Temperature:* 97.4

General: No apparent distress, appears stated age

Head, ear, eyes, nose, and throat: Marked swelling of the right cheek/parotid area with tenderness to palpation, no red streaks. Marked non-tender movable cervical lymphadenopathy

Cardiovascular: Regular rate and rhythm, no murmurs, rubs, or gallops

Chest: Clear to auscultation

Abdomen: Soft, normal, active bowel sounds, no hepatosplenomegaly

Musculo-skeletal: Full range of motion, no focal pain

Hospital Course: Upon admission, high-dose steroids were administered to shrink the gland. An otolaryngology consult was requested, and a bacterial culture of the gland was obtained. The patient's gland continued to swell, and she subsequently developed a facial cellulitis. A CT scan was performed, showing numerous abscesses in the parotid gland and inflammation tracking back to the sinus tracts. A PICC line was inserted for intravenous therapy. The patient improved on IV ciprofloxacin, Zosyn, and vancomycin. She received five days of intravenous therapy and is discharged on home antibiotic therapy to receive a total of ten days treatment. On discharge, the patient has been afebrile for 36 hours. The patient will follow up with otolaryngology and hematology in 3 days. ***Discharge Medications:*** Ciprofloxacin 500 mg po BID, Zosyn 3.375 grams IV q 6 hours, Solu-Medrol 125 mg IV q day, Dilaudid 4 mg po q 6 hours PRN pain, heparin flushes

All of the details in the discharge summary are accurate. None of the events or treatments seem particularly unreasonable or out of the ordinary. Still, a discharge summary is the reductio ad absurdum of medicine. Imagine a summary of *Romeo and Juliet: Boy meets girl. Families object. They kill themselves.* Reduced to its elements, the story has none of the tension, mystery, emotion, or moral wisdom of the play itself, with its elegant language and unforgettable characters. So, too, the discharge summary does not reflect the difficult decisions, false hopes, and disappointments that occur in any complicated illness. Nor does it reflect the individual human being upon whose body these events transpired. The fact that I am a doctor, albeit a new one, is not noted, although I thought my own knowledge might diminish the risk of errors. It did not, but it put me in a position to note all the stops and starts of the illness and its treatment, the mistakes and the flashes of insight, the humble heroes and the villains masquerading as saviors. In retrospect, I am able to see how disasters could have been averted, just as, given the chance, an audience who had seen the play would make sure that the letter from the kind apothecary saying that Juliet's suicide is faked would reach Romeo on time.

Here then, is the story of that same illness, from my point of view.

I was working at the pediatric emergency room in March when I came down with a bad cold. This was hardly a surprise. Several of the other interns and residents were sick. In the pediatric ER, kids with all sorts of viruses stream in and out, coughing and vomiting with abandon. Children are not polite when they are sick. They scream and wail. They throw things: bottles, french fries, applesauce. They do not cover their mouths when they cough. They sneeze explosively, and their spit and snot rain down in showers. One day the first kid I saw in the morning, a five-year-old named Gerald, spewed milk and orange Gatorade on me, and in a nice symmetry, the last patient of the day, a three-month-old named Maria, vomited over my shoulder and down my back.

Often you have to wrestle with children to examine them, and you may get kicked. It is best to position one holder at the head and one at the feet, and a third may be needed for the middle. One three-year-old girl, about 40 pounds, who had a corneal abrasion, required four holders, one of whom weighed 220 pounds and used to wrestle professionally. Even pinned and spread-eagled, she managed to free a little hand from under the plate-sized paw of one of the orderlies and scratch him. In desperate cases, when the child must be absolutely still, for a central line—an IV line inserted into one of the child's major veins—or for stitches, you can put him in a "papoose," which is a glorified straitjacket. Among all this "patient contact," it is impossible to avoid germs. I have no idea which of my tiny little foes gave me the virus—Maria, Gerald, Antonio with the drippy nose, Shaqueria, who stuck her pacifier in my eye, Ronald, whose mother forgot a spare diaper, Octavius, who coughed so hard he broke a rib—it could have come from any of them.

I got sick on the one weekend I was allowed off. It was to be my first weekend off in three months, and I had big plans for it: a movie, shopping for a new pair of shoes, dinner out with my husband. Interns are supposed to have every eighth day off, though in practice this doesn't always work out. We almost never get two days off in a row. If you have only a single day off, you usually just catch up on sleep, but two days—one day to catch up on sleep, and one that might actually be enjoyed!—are a rare luxury. Instead I spent both days in bed with nasal spray and Sudafed.

A cold affects me differently than other people. I am used to living with a certain level of discomfort. The medicines I take daily make me feel like I have a constant flu: muscle aches, woozy head, fatigue. My body has adjusted so that these feelings are baseline. If a stranger dropped into my body, he would probably complain that he felt sick, but to me this is everyday life.

Since I am always congested, the only difference when I get the flu is sneezing and a little fever. I passed the weekend with Kleenex and the VCR, and on Sunday night I was prepared to go back to work in the morning. But when I woke up, I discovered that overnight my lymph nodes had blossomed like fat roses. They ran in vines down my neck, my legs, and my arms. A riot of them filled my head so that I could not breathe. I called in sick.

When I first became chronically ill, back in college, my lymph nodes had blossomed the same way. The university infirmary had diagnosed mononucleosis, even when the mono tests were negative, but months went by and the nodes stayed swollen. I slept with my mouth agape, snoring like a steam horn. I was unable to hear unless someone yelled at me, because the glands blocked my ear canals. In class I sat in the front row, right below the professor, but if he turned to one side, I couldn't hear him. My notes were half-sentences and incomplete thoughts. These swollen nodes led to the second diagnosis of cancer, but ultimately they were explained by my chronically crazed immune system, desperately fighting a war it could not win. My lymph nodes were like the Maginot Line, big but useless. I lived with those swollen nodes for four years; then, when I started gamma globulin, they shrank from blossoms to buds.

I went to an internist at the university clinic, but she was at a loss as to how to help me. Seeing a new doctor can be tiring. I have to explain my condition all over again, what is known and what is not known. Usually the doctor ends up asking me what kind of treatment is appropriate. Having to help in this way is not unique to me as a doctor. Other people I know with immune deficiencies or rare medical problems frequently find themselves knowing more than the average primary care physician. Finally I suggested a combination of steroids and cough medicine. The steroids, I hoped, would shrink the glands; the cough medicine would help me sleep.

I began to feel guilty about missing work. When an intern is out sick, another intern gets called in. We all have the occasional true day off, and then we have "jeopardy days," when we must be available in case someone else is out. It is miserable to be called in on your jeopardy day. You feel singled out for misfortune by the gods. You think of the other interns, and it seems that they never get called in on jeopardy days. In fact, we all did. This was my first sick day of the year, and I did not feel horrible about taking one day, but two! And in my case, I never know if one sick day is going to turn into a week of illness or a month, or if it is going to change my life forever. I was determined to go in the next day, and I went to bed at nine o'clock.

I woke up at 3 a.m. with a familiar ache in my face. In the darkness, I reached up to feel my jaw, then stumbled into the bathroom to look in the mirror. The right side of my face had inflated like a balloon. I had an infection in my one remaining parotid gland. It had been seven years since my last infection, and I had truly believed that as long as I received my gamma globulin I would never have another. This one didn't feel like a relapse, since I had never felt cured, but it felt like another battle lost in the war: first the lymph nodes, now the parotid gland. The truce with my aberrant lymphocytes was falling apart. The troops had smashed through interferon and antibodies. And my faulty immune system had sat quietly by while the city was ravaged.

I was scared. I turned off the light so I didn't have to see my swollen face. I wrapped myself in a blanket and pressed a hot washcloth to my face. I thought in this early stage perhaps I could just press the gland back down. It felt thick and meaty, and when I pressed it, a tiny drop of salty saliva leaked out, followed by a sharp contraction, like a nutcracker makes. I cut open a lemon and began to lick it. Sour things make saliva flow through the gland and stimulate drainage. I sat, licking lemons, with a hot compress to my face, until seven o'clock. Then I called and said I wouldn't be coming to work again. At nine I called Dr. Charlotte Cunningham-Rundles, my immunologist, in New York. She was sympathetic to my discomfort, but we'd been through this infection seven times before. Sometimes it would resolve with rest and antibiotics alone. I did not always have to go into the hospital. She recommended I get a culture of the gland's secretions. Immune-deficient patients are prone to both run-of-the-mill and oddball infections. She thought it worthwhile to find out what bug was causing these recurrent problems.

I phoned the doctor on call and spoke with a nurse about obtaining the bacterial culture. The nurse recognized my name; she had gotten to know me through the years and was amazed to learn that I was now an intern, finished with medical school. "Where does the time go?" she asked before she put me on hold. When she came back to the phone, she told me that the doctor did not have time to see me.

"It's important," I told her.

She sighed. "Let me get him."

I waited on the phone, holding the receiver in one hand and a warm compress in the other.

"Hello, Jamie," the doctor said.

I started to explain the situation to him. He interrupted. Parotid infections, he said, are always caused by one of two organisms. He repeated that he had no time to see me and said, "I'll call in some antibiotics. Go buy some lemon drops to suck on."

I explained that because of my immune deficiency I was prone to unusual infections, but he dismissed me. "Not in the parotid." Then he said, "Look, I've got a really busy clinic. Patients waiting. Give the nurse your pharmacy number and tell her what antibiotic you want, and she'll call it in. Or," he said, "you can call it in yourself. I understand you're a doctor now."

Somehow he had managed to turn the fact that I was a doctor back on me. He made it clear that he was not required to listen to my opinion; in fact, he implied, I should know better than to bother him. If I was a doctor, I should call the medicine in myself. I was only eight months into training, an intern, the lowest on the totem pole of the hospital hierarchy, and I was so used to clear and covert insinuations of ignorance that the doctor's condescending tone was not immediately apparent to me. He knew more than I, he said, and he implied that it was out of ignorance alone that I was calling him with petty questions and requests.

I ended up telling the nurse the name of the antibiotic I had used for previous parotid infections, and she called the pharmacy.

Victor, my husband, picked up the medicine, along with a real heating pad and some lemon drops. I trundled back to bed to try the ancient cure of rest and fluids. I sucked on a lemon drop, and my whole face contracted.

Patients with chronic conditions develop an unusual combination of battle weariness and post-traumatic stress disorder. On the one hand, we are tough and cynical. We shovel snow with fevers. We walk around with scars and deformities. We tell nurses where to find the best veins, and if they can't find them, we poke needles intrepidly into our own flesh. We accept that at least a little bit of pain is the price of our existence. On the other hand, along with pain, we live with a baseline of fear. We know that any infection can turn life-threatening. We know that ICU stands both for Intensive Care Unit and In Case U might die. We know how quickly the body can turn, from human to something else entirely, something whipped and beaten, sniveling and gashed and torn by pain. With a mixture of gallantry and fear, I waited for my body to decide where it was going to take me. I tried to read a novel. I tried to watch TV, but there was nothing on: talk shows with sobbing guests confessing to mundane sins, a cooking show that made me queasy, the Teletubbies.

I tried to write but couldn't concentrate. I got in bed and stared at the ceiling.

By the afternoon, my body was declaring itself. I began to shake and sweat. The side of my face where the gland sits had grown larger and had turned a mottled red, partly from infection and partly from the heating pad. I took my temperature—102 degrees. I called the doctor again. I told him I had a fever and shaking chills.

He said, "You know as well as I do that there are lots of reasons to have fevers and chills." Again, he managed to turn the fact that I had any medical knowledge back around on me, implying that I should have learned in medical school that this was not a dangerous situation. In fact, I learned the opposite in medical school. Fever and chills in an immune-deficient patient is a very dangerous situation indeed. Of course, I knew this fact already as a patient, but I had four years of school, eight months of training, and two national board exams to back me up. Still, he made me doubt everything I knew. I played intern to his attending, patient to his doctor.

He sighed with frustration. "Keep doing what you're doing," he said. "If you don't feel better tomorrow, maybe we can squeeze you into the schedule." He hung up.

I was nervous. This infection was following the pattern of the first parotid infection, when I had wound up at Massachusetts General with a fever of 105 degrees, flat on my face on the hospital floor. I did not want to be that sick again. I forced myself to eat another lemon drop, as if the punishment of the pain could heal me.

I continued to worsen. I was unable to swallow any soup. My face felt at once squeezed and stretched. In desperation I called the answering service, hoping perhaps someone else was on call and would understand the urgency of the situation. No such luck. They paged the same doctor for me. He called me back after a few minutes. He made no attempt to hide his irritation. I told him things were getting worse.

"You can't make it until tomorrow?" he asked incredulously.

"I'm not sure. I don't want to be septic."

"Well," he sighed. "I'm not going to the hospital to see you. I'm watching my kids; my wife is out of town. But if you insist on being admitted, I'll call the resident and tell her to go in."

"I think it would be better," I told him.

"Fine." He hung up.

At first I was shocked rather than angry. Most doctors, for fear of a lawsuit if nothing else, will send their patients to be evaluated for a fever. Despite my repeated reminders of my compromised immune system and of past serious illnesses, the doctor had treated me like a nagging hypochondriac and a terrible inconvenience. There are such patients, perfectly healthy people who treat the hospital like a vacation, an escape from work or family, who call their doctors daily with concerns about the number of bowel movements they are having or the fact that the neighbor's kid has strep throat or the feeling that their heart is racing, who demand narcotics and constant attention. But I did not know how I had earned such a characterization. Before that day, I'd never made a single after-hours call.

I put a nightshirt, a toothbrush, some soap, an extra towel, a pair of slippers, and a book into a bag. I've been in the hospital enough times to know what I need. They provide toothbrushes, but the bristles are too hard. The slippers don't fit my feet, and they give you little towels, coarse from too much washing and bleaching. I packed slowly in order to give the resident time to reach the hospital before me and

look over my chart. I knew it would be an unpleasant call.
No one likes to have to leave home and go into the hospital for an emergency admission. But at least it was only
8 p.m. Middle-of-the-night calls are worse. Then suddenly I
got angry. What the hell was the doctor doing watching his
kids if he was on call? I had been far too understanding all
day. He had been irresponsible, arrogant, and lazy. If I had
not insisted on going to the hospital, I might easily have become gravely ill. In the past, I'd come close to dying. He
would have been inexcusably at fault if that happened. Ironically, my own medical knowledge saved him from disaster,
although there was incompetence yet to come.

The ER was packed that night. I signed in and wrote next
to my name "scheduled admit." Then I sat down to wait,
with my blue gelatinous heating pad and my bag of lemon
drops. My head was now swelled up like a lopsided balloon. The only relief from the pain came from the heating
pad, and Victor had to stand in line to reheat it in the mi-
crowave, behind people with Styrofoam cups of tea and coffee. No one called me to take vital signs, but I did not want
to pull rank as house staff of the hospital and demand to be
seen. It seemed unfair to the other sick people.

Waiting rooms are filled with a curious mix of despair and
boredom. Reels of CNN play, rewind, and start over, as if
time were limited to two hours. The waiting room has its
own hierarchy; the sickest are at the top of the list. High status is demonstrated by arriving in an ambulance, not a lim-
ousine. Illness is a great equalizer, and in the ER a convict
with a gunshot wound outranks Bill Gates with a splinter.

The character of the room varies from hospital to hospital,
but at Emory, a university hospital, there were all classes
and races. A Vietnamese family sat in one corner: a mother,
a father, two children, and a baby. I couldn't tell who was

sick—or perhaps the sick person had already been whisked away. An older man—obviously on chemotherapy, judging from his bald head and his pallor—kneaded his wife's hand. Another man, all alone, kept turning away from us and covering his ear while he talked on a cellular phone, although the room was really very quiet. Once in a while, a door opened; a name was called, and a single person—or, more often, a group—shuffled across the room. Usually all but the patient and one other person were turned back, and then the rejected family members settled themselves back into the vinyl chairs, cast their eyes up to CNN or over toward the clock, and waited for time to pass.

Doctors rarely venture into the waiting room. When I am working in the ER, by the time I see a patient the nurses have already called him back, put in the IV, and taken the vitals. He is in a flimsy green hospital gown, and a plastic bag labeled "patient belongings" lies at his feet. It's as if he's joined an odd sort of army; he's been given his uniform and stripped of the things that define him. I don't know if he wears sneakers or boots or loafers. I don't know if she arrived in a dress or sweatpants or a housecoat. There may be a family member, even two, with the patient, but if an entourage is waiting, I am unaware of them. As I sat in the ER waiting room, it occurred to me that although I had spent long stretches of days and nights in the Emory ER itself, I had never before seen this room, with its mustard-colored carpeting and artificial plants and patients caught in the first moments of illness, still in their street clothes.

An hour passed, and it seemed odd that the resident had not come looking for me. My parents arrived. I had told them it was not necessary to come, but they were worried. My father was surprised to find me still in the waiting room. I went back into the actual emergency room, where I had worked many long nights. Ernest, a resident I knew from medical school, was there. He was shocked at the sight of my face. He had no idea I had an immune deficiency, and parotid infections are very rare in young people. He told me they'd get me back right away, but I explained that this was a scheduled admission and asked if he had seen the resident I was to meet there.

He said all admissions went through the ER, and he'd heard nothing about it. He checked the log to confirm his impression. Then he said he'd page the resident himself. I went back to the waiting room.

A minute later Ernest called my name. I met him at the door that separated the waiting room from the ER proper. He said the resident had been told nothing of my admission.

"What?" I asked. I could feel my face getting redder.

"She happens to be here seeing another patient," he said, "but no one called her."

Not only had the doctor refused to see me earlier in the day, not only had he condescendingly refused to acknowledge that I might know something about appropriate care for myself, not only had he guiltlessly admitted that, although he was on call, he could not come to the hospital; he had not even picked up the phone and dialed the ten digits to page the resident. It was his fault I was left stranded in that crowded waiting room, when I should have been in a hospital bed receiving IV antibiotics. I half-wished I would die, so that Victor could sue the pants off him and strip him of his license to practice medicine.

Ernest said, "She's seeing a patient. She'll be down when she's done." He touched the side of my face. "Dr. Grist is here, too. Maybe we should have him look at you."

At the mention of Dr. Grist's name, I felt almost as if Dr. Gussack were still with me. They had been partners, and before he died, Dr. Gussack told me to see Dr. Grist if I ever needed surgery again.

A short time later Dr. Grist arrived. I had not seen him since Dr. Gussack's memorial service. He and his family had sat in front of me and my parents, and I remembered noticing the crystal-white hair of his children. I also remember that his voice cracked when he stood up to speak, and when he sat back down, he dropped his head in his hands and sighed. He does not look anything like Dr. Gussack. Dr. Gussack was neat and compact and always had on a beautiful tie. Dr. Grist looks like he just flew out the door. He is tall and reedy, an Ichabod Crane with a haystack of hair.

Dr. Grist took one look at my face and said, "Of course you need to be admitted right away."

He introduced himself to Victor and my parents. Then he walked with us to the eighth floor of the hospital. He went to write orders, and I crawled into bed. It was late. A nurse came in and started an IV. Dr. Grist returned and told me which antibiotic he had chosen. He asked me if, in the past, any unusual organisms had caused my parotitis, recognizing as the other doctor had not that immune-deficient patients are prone to such problems. I told him that I was not aware of any and that in this case we would never know, as the other doctor had failed to do a culture. (Once you have taken antibiotics—and I'd already had two doses—most cultures will not grow.)

The failure to get a bacterial culture that day was the first step in a devastating series of events. Without knowing the organism, we were left fighting blindly, throwing antibiotics like missiles at an unidentified target. Of course, I didn't know that night what a terrible mistake had been made. Like a soldier pulled from battle, unaware of his wounds, I just felt grateful that finally someone was taking care of me. The nurse came back in and delivered a painkiller through the IV. I fell asleep in the middle of saying good-night.

I left the hospital after two days of IV antibiotics and went home on pills. The swelling was only slightly diminished, but the pain was gone, and I no longer had a fever. Dr. Grist and I had decided that the gland would have to be removed, but he wanted to wait until the infection and inflammation had resolved. It is difficult, he explained, to visualize the facial nerve in an inflamed gland because the angry gland makes everything—nerves, blood vessels, and glandular tissue—look the same. It is of the utmost importance to be able to visualize the nerve in order to avoid cutting it and thus paralyzing the patient's face. I was concerned that the gland would never shrink back to its preinfection size. After the last parotid infection, the gland on the left had stayed swollen, though it went from soft and fleshy to hard and ropy. The swelling had made it particularly difficult to remove, and I did not want to present such a challenging case again. I wanted to shrink the gland.

After some discussion with Dr. Grist and Dr. Cunningham-Rundles, I was started on oral corticosteroids, prednisone. Corticosteroids are anti-inflammatory medications used to treat everything from poison ivy to multiple sclerosis. In my case, we were using them to destroy some of the white blood cells that were clogging the parotid gland.

Unfortunately, I failed to make clear to Dr. Cunningham-Rundles, who was trying to help me long distance from New York City—free of charge—that I continued to take steroids after completing the course of antibiotics. In this case, I believe, I contributed my own serious medical error. It had been my idea, as a fledgling doctor, to take the steroids. A more experienced doctor would recognize that once I stopped antibiotics, if I continued to take the immune-suppressing steroids, I was a setup for relapse or reinfection. Dr. Cunningham-Rundles could not examine me, nor did she have the opportunity to look at my chart. And so this one small fact fell through the cracks. I would not call this medical error; it was simply a problem of logistics, brought on by my having a condition so obscure that no one in Atlanta felt confident managing the case.

I went back to work. I was scheduled for a month in the emergency room of the city hospital, where I would be exposed to pneumonia, tuberculosis, cytomegalovirus, chicken pox, and a whole host of other pathogens. The hematologist who was caring for me felt that such exposures would be too dangerous for me, given the fact that I was on high-dose steroids. She called the chief resident, and I was switched to the bone marrow transplant service, where the patients were actually more immuno-suppressed than I. After ten days, however, despite the sterile environment, I was back in the hospital.

The gland, which had initially shrunk, was growing again, blooming like a bright, waxy tulip. This time I did not go through the emergency room. The hematologist called hospital admissions, and I checked in as if I were going to a hotel. I signed my name to a list, then sat down. I had brought my knitting. The ubiquitous CNN was on. A young woman sat with her basketball coach, waiting to be admitted for an evaluation of back pain. Another woman and her husband whispered quietly to each other. She asked me what I was making, and when I told her it was a sweater for my husband, she looked sad and said, "I never did learn to knit." She watched my hands move. I could tell she wanted to talk, so I asked her why she was coming to the hospital.

"Oh," she said, almost as if she were surprised that I knew she was in the hospital. "He"—she placed a hand on her husband's shoulder, but he did not look at her—"is being evaluated for a heart transplant."

When my name was called, I answered some questions, signed some forms, probably promising my firstborn child if insurance failed to pay. The receptionist asked me if I wanted a wheelchair to take me to my room. I looked askance at her. That morning I'd been rounding on patients in this very hospital. "No thanks," I said. "I'll walk."

I was happy to be on the sixth floor, where I'd worked as an intern. I knew the nurses there; they were all excellent and kind. I knew they'd be able to get an IV into my thready veins. If I was going to have to be in the hospital, at least I would be among friends. The resident on service came to write the history and physical. It was Eric, a freckle-faced young man with a Southern drawl whom I knew from a previous rotation at the VA. He winced at the sight of my swollen face, but I assured him it looked worse than it was. Once again I saw that quizzical look when someone who thinks they know the basic facts of you realizes there is a whole other dimension—not pity but wonder, as if I'd announced that I was a nun or a prizefighter. I explained my condition to him, essentially filling out the history and physical for him. He blushed the whole way through. We were colleagues, and it was as if I were confiding the details of my marriage to him instead of the details of my viscera. He did an awkward, hasty physical exam on me: listened to the lungs, heart, and abdomen through my shirt. I looked straight ahead and tried to give the impression that in this context he could touch my body without touching me. Neither of us was convinced. He skipped feeling the spleen and liver, and I thought again what intimate acts we perform on patients, much easier to do on strangers than on friends. He went to write my admission orders.

Admission orders for all patients follow a basic pattern. As a medical student, you learn the mnemonic: ADC VANDaLISM. A for admit to floor. D for diagnosis: pneumonia, lung cancer, schizophrenia. C for condition: stable, guarded, fair. V for how often to take vital signs: every two hours in the ICU, every shift on the floor. A for drug allergies. N for special nursing care: walking the patient, patient confined to bedrest, restraints, isolation. D for diet: regular, diabetic, no food at all. L is for labs you want drawn, and I is for IV fluids. S is for special care, for example, visits from the respiratory therapist, and M is for medications. For some of the chronically ill, those with a combination of problems—for example, heart disease, diabetes, and hypertension (a common triad)—the list of medications can run a whole page. For me, there were only two medicines: an antibiotic and a steroid. I had brought my own interferon since I prefer to give the subcutaneous shots myself.

The otolaryngologists were asked to advise on the management of parotitis. Dr. Grist was out of town, unfortunately. The attending physician did not know me at all, but he followed routine protocol for a swollen parotid gland. He sent the resident to get a bacterial culture. The resident, Dave, had the ruffled appearance of many surgical residents, a five o'clock shadow, loosely tied scrubs, and ragged blue paper shoe covers on his feet that he'd worn right out of the operating room. He introduced himself and told me he was going to have to extract fluid from my swollen gland. A culture swab was sticking out of the back pocket of his scrub pants.

I opened my mouth as wide as the swelling would allow, and he put the tube inside, against the cheek where the parotid duct opens. He pressed hard—squeezed and mashed—on my swollen face, trying to push fluid through the jammed, tortuous twists of the parotid duct. It felt as if he were trying to wring the last drop of water from my face. He tightened and tightened, twisting and pulling my face until I feared it would tear. Finally he withdrew the tip of the swab. He looked at it and said only, "It's pus." That meant there was an infection; a bacterium there, a smart one, had outlived the slings and arrows of two powerful antibiotics. It meant also that I was not infected with garden variety staph or strep, as the first doctor had insisted. Those organisms would have been killed by the antibiotics I received. I had a different kind of bug, one that should have been identified two weeks ago, on the very first day I got sick, when I begged the doctor to do the culture.

Dave glanced at me, dropped a hand on the bed, and said, "Sorry that hurt."

After Dave left, I tried to read. I had not changed into a hospital gown. Putting on a gown always seems like a concession to me. If I can avoid the gown and Jell-O consumption, I still have one foot in the world of the healthy. I refused to get into bed in the middle of the day. I sat in the chair for visitors. Later the hematology attending and fellow came to see me. I had worked with both of them before, and we had a friendly chat. Victor came to visit, and I had to give up the chair for the bed. I was beginning to feel a little more ill than I had that morning, when I checked in, but I thought most of that was hospital humdrums. At five o'clock dinner appeared. I rejected the green Jell-O, pushed around the amorphous mass that was reputed to be turkey and gravy, and drank the apple juice. At six o'clock my parents arrived.

My father wanted to know what was planned. I told him IV steroids and vancomycin. I realized then that I had not yet received the antibiotics that had been ordered at least six hours earlier. My father was angry, but I told him they would surely arrive soon. Meanwhile I glanced in the mirror and saw that my face was much more swollen than it had been that morning. It was starting to ache, and although I'd refused painkillers before, I asked for them now. Another half hour passed; still no antibiotics. Victor went to the nurses' station to inquire. The nurse paged the attending, who came to my room with the staff pharmacist. The attending was shocked to learn that the antibiotics had not been given. She asked the pharmacist how six hours could pass without an ordered antibiotic being administered. Six hours is critical in a patient with a serious infection. Six hours could send you to the intensive care unit; six hours could allow the infection to spread to the brain; in six hours you could die.

The pharmacist did not have an explanation for the delay. He shuffled his feet, looked at the floor, and said, "You didn't order them stat."

Stat means something has to be given or done right away, immediately, that very second. If a patient is having a seizure, we order Ativan stat, because we want it given that moment, not five minutes later. If a patient complains of chest pain, we order a stat EKG; difficulty breathing, a stat pulse oximetry to measure blood oxygen. When an antibiotic is ordered, it should be given within one or two hours, unless it is ordered stat—in which case it should be given immediately. Waiting six hours to hang an antibiotic is a clear-cut medical error. There would be no defense in a courtroom.

As it turned out later, vancomycin would not have treated my infection, and so the pharmacist's failure to deliver the medication to me had no consequences. In this case, a blatant mistake was committed, but unlike the failure to obtain a bacterial culture, it had no effect on outcome. I would venture to say that such inconsequential errors might be the most common kinds of medical mistakes; they occur with alarming frequency. For every error that has consequences, there are probably a hundred that have none, and they are never noted or recorded. In any event, such sloppiness is more forgivable than laziness and arrogance.

The pharmacist walked out of the room without looking at me or apologizing, and the antibiotic was delivered fifteen minutes later. It did not help. My face continued to swell, and it started to hurt, a stretched-out, muddy pain, as if hot hands were grasping my face, molding it like clay, shaping and reshaping it but unable to find a satisfactory form. The nurse gave me some morphine, and I fell asleep for a while. Some time later an orderly woke me to go down to radiology for a CT scan. I was dizzy from the morphine, and the pain was starting to overwhelm me. I was unsteady on my feet, so I had to sit in a wheelchair. My father pushed me.

The radiology room was empty except for two nurses. Behind a curtain, I saw the slippered feet of a man on a stretcher and heard the rhythmic push and sigh of a ventilator. The lights were bright, and the linoleum floor almost glowed. The room was very clean and hollow, and the nurse who sat beside me smelled soapy. She decided the IV in my arm was too small for the contrast dye that would be infused in order to visualize the blood vessels. My father told her she would never get an IV in me, certainly not a large one. She insisted on trying. I held out my arms for her; she put the tourniquet on tight and jabbed the needle first into one vein, then another. A sharp pain shot up my arm and for a moment distracted me from the throbbing moon that had replaced my head. She dug the needle down and muttered, "I know it's in here somewhere," as if my vein were a bad little boy, hiding from a well-deserved punishment. The needle nosed deeper but never found its target. She did not succeed in getting an IV in, but she did succeed in giving me two large, symmetrical purple bruises. My parents looked away. I apologized to her. "I'm a hard stick."

She gave up. The contrast was delivered through the IV I already had. Contrast dye makes the whole body flush; you get a metallic taste in your mouth, and you feel like you're falling. These odd sensations are universal, and the nurses warn you they are coming. The heat you feel is unlike any other kind of heat, not the feeling of running on a hot day or sitting in front of a fire or basking in the sun. It is combustible. It radiates from the inside out and makes you strangely aware that you have an inside. Then it passes.

I was brought back to the scanner alone. An orderly helped me lie on the narrow, cold table. My head had been raised all day. When I put my head down, the pain suddenly rushed in, wave after wave of it. It poured in and kept pouring in, a flood of it that continued even after my head was full. I asked for more morphine. They told me they didn't give morphine in radiology.

"I can't do this," I said.

"We'll take you back upstairs."

I knew the scan was important. We had to see how far the infection had spread. So I steeled myself.

The technicians and the orderly skirted into a glass room

and left me alone in darkness. There was a buzz, and the table shifted back into the doughnut ring of the scanner.

"Take a breath," a godlike voice whispered out of nowhere.

The scanner whirred.

"Breathe," the voice commanded. "Deep breath." More whirring. The scanner was a watery blue color with a red laser dot in the center. The laser clicked and winked like a false eye.

"We're done," the voice declared, and the glass door opened and light streamed in as if a spell had been broken. The technician, a young woman with her blond hair in a braid, said, "Good job." The orderly rolled me off the table and back into the wheelchair. My parents wheeled me upstairs.

As soon as I was back in bed, I called for more morphine. I wanted to forget about my head, but the hot hands of pain were back, pushing and pulling on my cheeks and ears. I rang for the nurse and croaked, "Morphine," into the intercom. When the nurse came with the morphine, I felt the pain—and my head with it—float away, like those astronauts, untethered from the mother ship, drifting into infinity. I told my parents to go home, as I was falling asleep.

I woke up an hour later. My head had found its way back, and it was angry, alternately pushing and clawing at me. Victor had gone to get dinner while I was in the CT scanner. Now he was back. I saw him blurrily. I pushed the call button for the nurse and asked for more painkillers.

Victor looked at me, worried and confused.

The nurse, Jane, appeared in the doorway in her pink nurse's scrubs. She stood by my bed and said softly, "Honey, you just had some."

"I need more," I begged.

"Let me see," she said.

Jane returned with a small dose of morphine. "This is all I can give you, honey."

I could not tell I'd been given anything at all.

"Please, Jane, please," I begged her. She shook her head.

I truly cannot find the words to describe the pain, partly because I cannot fully remember it but more because it was an experience unlike any other. I can say something was the color and taste of a strawberry or had the smell of old wood because these sensations can be shared, but I have never before felt the kind of excruciating pain that trapped me that night. I do not know the pain of a gunshot wound or a heart attack, of a burst appendix or metastatic cancer. Perhaps if I knew one of those pains, I could compare it to my pain that night, but then it would have meaning only for those who had suffered those agonies. And even so we would all look back at our pain from the great distance of having survived it. When you are done, when the pain lifts, you leave it behind. You walk away and don't look back. You never know what happened to it: Was it swallowed by time? Did it wash out to sea? Did it leap into another body, or did it just dissolve?

I have seen patients in terrible pain, patients so lost in their pain that they have no present, no consciousness. In such cases, doctors find themselves treating the pain rather than the patient, as if some horrible monster had entered the room and must be pushed away, outside, down the stairs, out the window. The patient is gone, but the moaning persists, the moaning that is the final veil between life and death, and that seems to tell us that what is coming is not beautiful but terrible, not calm but a ceaseless squall. The point becomes not the patient's comfort but the patient's quiet, as if silence were the same thing as painlessness.

Jane did everything she could to quiet me. She paged the intern on call, but all he offered were some pills. I have been that intern, called to minister to an unknown patient. Like him, I have been reluctant to prescribe strong narcotics, unsure if the pain is real. Of course, had the intern come to my bedside that night, he might have been less cautious. My face was swollen like an angry Picasso. My mouth gaped open, my right eye twisted up to my forehead. I could not swallow a pill. I moaned and pressed my swollen face into the heating pad, hoping to burn it off. I rang for Jane every few minutes because I had no sense of time, but Jane was limited in what she could do. Only doctors can prescribe pain medicine, even though the nurse often has a much greater appreciation of the patient's condition. She must follow what is written on the chart or the few concessions that an intern might make over the telephone. When I asked for more morphine, Jane would tell me quietly that she couldn't give me any more. She'd just given me IV morphine half an hour before. I had to wait two and a half hours for more. I couldn't do it. I told her to let me die, please let me die. If someone had rolled me to the window, I would have jumped; I was so gripped with pain, so rolled up and tangled in it, that I could not imagine any pleasure that could outweigh this agony. I would trade it all, my entire future, children and grandchildren, vacations at the beach, the view from the top of the Eiffel Tower, birthday parties, new car smells, Thanksgiving Day, for relief from this torture.

Victor sat helplessly next to my bed.

Jane could not watch me suffer; sometime after midnight she called the pain service, woke the attending physician, and said I had to be seen. The pain service is a relatively new entity in most hospitals, brought on by the development of new pain control techniques and increasing awareness that patients' pain is often undertreated. The service is made up of a group of anesthesiologists, physician's assistants, and nurse practitioners whose sole job is to manage and care for patients in pain. Depending on the situation, the patient may have an epidural placed, or he may be prescribed IV medication, sometimes through a special IV pump called a PCA pump, for "patient-controlled anesthesia," which enables the patient to press a button and deliver to himself a set amount of pain medicine every few minutes. In other cases, oral medication is given, including methadone, which is used in some patients with long-term pain control problems.

Dr. Hammonds, an anesthesiologist, came to see me that night. Although I am eternally grateful to him, I have no idea what he looks like. Victor says that I spoke coherently to him, that I explained that I was an intern and even used appropriate medical terms, but I remember nothing. It is possible, even probable, that they gave me some medicine to make me forget the previous few hours.

Dr. Hammonds ordered a pump containing IV Dilaudid, the most powerful opiate painkiller. I pressed a button, and the pump delivered a dose of it straight to my veins. It put me on another planet. I remember still being vaguely aware that I hurt but not recognizing the sensation and not really caring. This is the basic mechanism of narcotic painkillers. They do not interrupt the actual signal to the brain: the pain nerves are still triggered and firing. But other nerves are also activated, and these nerves somehow render the pain inconsequential and unimportant. In the case of addiction, it seems, this mechanism works not only for physiological but also for psychological pain. Our failures and disappointments, memories and regrets, no longer matter. If asked, I would have placed little or no value on the things I normally treasured: books and art, gardens and oceans, even my family all sort of hovered around me, recognized but insubstantial, like a cloud. But I was not in pain, no longer immersed in a bubbling vat of agony. Yet while Plato says pleasure is the absence of pain, I would not say that what I felt at that moment was pleasure. I floated between the two, not human enough to feel either.

When I woke up in the morning, my head was rubbery. I felt a sharp twist in my cheek, but when I pressed the button on my PCA pump, it settled down like a scolded dog. I stood to go to the bathroom and saw myself in the mirror. My head was enormous, a half-rotten pumpkin planted on my shoulders. The right side was pulled up and out like taffy. My eye angled up, and my jaw swung open. The skin was red from sleeping on a heating pad, and red streaks of infection splayed up and over my eyes and swollen cheeks as if a giant had slapped me. I touched my face, and it was entirely unfamiliar.

Jane came into the room to check on me. I thanked her for helping me. She said, "You'll get better, sweetie. The worst is over." Then she apologized for not always coming as quickly as she should have. While she had been trying to relieve my pain, another of her patients that night had been dying of cancer. It was her job to make that death painless— or at least quiet. Although I had begged to die the night before, I realized that I was lucky to be still among the living.

Later that day the infectious disease service came to see me. Dr. Helmut Albrecht knocked on the door. I knew Dr. Albrecht from a lecture he had given. In Germany he had been an attending physician; I heard he'd run an HIV clinic.

He had come to America to do an infectious disease fellow-ship. He was one of the better-known fellows, partly be-cause he is very smart and partly because he is very handsome. Again, I remember very little of this meeting. Dr. Albrecht had examined my chart and my CT scan. He asked me a few questions. Again, I reportedly explained what was known of my immune deficiency. He told me that my white count had reached a critical level: 42,000. (The high end of normal is 8,000.) At this level, the lab calls the floor with the results immediately—another precaution, in case the nurses and doctors forget to check the lab values or do not do so in an expedient fashion. A white count over 30,000 usually means a patient is at risk for going into shock, dropping her blood pressure to a point where not enough blood reaches the brain to maintain consciousness, the kidneys shut down, and the liver dies; in doctor terms, multisystem organ failure. Dr. Albrecht was very concerned about this white count and my continued fever.

He also explained that I had a facial cellulitis, an infection of the soft tissue of my face, and that the infection was only a few millimeters from my sinus tracts. I knew what that meant. The sinus tracts lead directly back to the brain. They are one of the notorious flaws in the design of the human body. Though the precious brain is encased in the thick bones of the skull and then is wrapped in three protective layers known as the meninges, an infection that finds it way into the sinus tracts can march unimpeded directly to the central nervous system. If my infection reached my brain, it could lead to, at best, a brain abscess; it could also leave me paralyzed, mute, amnesiac, or brain damaged, or it might kill me.

The CT scan from the night before had shown that my parotid gland was filled with dozens of filmy bubbles. Although he did not bring it up, I realized as Dr. Albrecht talked that this terrible infection, and the attendant pain, would not have occurred if the ENT resident had not struggled so assiduously to obtain a bacterial culture the day before. Bacteria percolated inside each bubble. When the resident squeezed my face, the bubbles burst, and the liberated bacteria streamed up my face and down my neck, into my blood, and now they were rapidly marching toward my brain. In one almost imperceptible turn, the resident had steered my illness toward disaster. Yet in a strict sense, his insistence on obtaining a culture was not a mistake. It was certainly not as reproachable as the first doctor's refusal to obtain a culture. In fact, it served to underscore the gravity of that refusal. Good results from an early culture would have made the second one unnecessary. But the resident was just following the attending's orders. I was treated like a standard patient: cultures should be obtained prior to treating parotitis. Neither the attending nor the resident considered the possible consequences of getting a culture, that I might have an abscess that could burst, that the culture might in the end do more harm than good. Before the culture had a chance to grow and offer any valuable information (it usually takes forty-eight hours before a bacteria can be identified in the laboratory), my illness became critical.

Dr. Albrecht could only guess at which antibiotics to use. One thing was certain: the infection was not caused by staph or strep, because it raged on despite the vancomycin, an antibiotic that should kill those organisms. Working blindly, Dr. Albrecht ordered two additional intravenous antibiotics to cover many more kinds of bacteria and to be given stat, immediately.

The rest of the day passed in an opiate haze. Friends—other residents and interns—came to see me and chatted politely. Only one person faltered when he first walked into the room. He saw me notice this and apologized. "I'm sorry," he said. "It just looks like it hurts so much."

I nodded my pumpkin head and gaily waved at the pump that delivered my painkillers. "That's why I have this," I said.

I began to feel better on the new antibiotics, even though my face stayed swollen. I drifted in and out of the day. I was so drugged that the nurse was scared I'd fall down if I walked to the bathroom. She brought a portable commode that I used without modesty.

Late in the afternoon, the attending infectious disease doctor, Dr. M, came to see me. He explained that the culture had grown only normal mouth flora. He believed that these organisms were the infecting bacteria, and for this reason I did not need three different antibiotics. I needed only one. I was too drugged to argue with him. Shortly after he left the room, the antibiotics Dr. Albrecht had ordered were removed.

Once more a decision had been made which, in hindsight, might look like a mistake. When we choose antibiotics with which to treat our patients, we are often guessing. We start the medications before a culture has had a chance to grow, and so we base our choice on what we know from other patients. Certain bacteria live in the mouth; others live in the bowel, the genitourinary tract, the ear. Dr. M chose an antibiotic on the basis of what he knew from past experience and from textbooks; he did not think that my immune deficiency would have a significant impact. There are risks to using too many antibiotics. That allows antibiotic-resistant bacteria to grow in the body, and some of the medications may have serious side effects, from renal failure to destruction of the liver. Dr. M made a judgment call. He chose to minimize the possible risk of medications, but he also left himself little room for error. The antibiotic he ordered treated only a narrow subset of infections; if an unusual bacterium was growing in my body, it would continue unchecked.

When my parents came, I explained to them what had happened. My father looked at my temperature chart and saw that while it had fallen on Dr. Albrecht's antibiotics, the last reading was high again. Worse still, red lines were spidering across my face again. We both knew that fevers often drop in the morning, and so the change of antibiotics might have nothing to do with the temperature spike, but the red lines were harbingers of a spreading infection. My father told the nurse he wanted to ask the infectious disease attending some questions.

Dr. M entered the room with a smile. My mother and father were in the only two chairs, so he leaned against a wall, with his arms crossed. He calmly explained that the bacteria culture showed only mouth flora, and he believed the culture to be accurate. Therefore he had chosen the most appropriate antibiotic. My father pointed out that the culture could be wrong.

"I don't think it is," Dr. M said.

"But if it is," my father insisted, "it could be very dangerous."

"There's no reason to think that it is," Dr. M repeated.

"She's not feeling as well."

"That can't be due to the drugs. Not enough time has passed."

"Her temperature's up."

"But not enough time has passed," Dr. M said calmly, "for the antibiotics to be responsible. Temperatures fluctuate," he said, almost musing.

"I want her on the other drugs," my father declared.

"She doesn't need them. The drug I have chosen will treat her infection."

Finally I spoke up. "I think I need broader coverage. I think it would be better."

"You do not at all need it."

"I want it."

Dr. M shrugged. "If you insist, I'll tell Dr. Albrecht to order the other antibiotics," he said. But he repeated, "You do not need them."

The problem with medicine—and the reason the field is inherently prone to errors—is that while we learn by memorization and multiple choice, our patients are never as clearly defined as the proverbial textbook case. If you miss a question on an exam, nothing happens to your paper patient, and after the exam you can look up the correct answer. But each decision on a live patient occurs in the linear and unchangeable sequence of time that confines human life. There is no going back. The results of your decision—good or bad—crash and tumble, often cascading beyond your control. By ordering the extra antibiotics, Dr. Albrecht might have been using a rifle to kill a fly, but since, as it turned out, the fly alone would be hurt and I would be saved, I do not view this as an error at all.

I will never know who was right in this dispute. I do know this: with all three antibiotics, I got better. My white blood cell count dropped almost to normal in forty-eight hours. My fever broke, and a repeat CT scan showed the infection retreating. Maybe I also would have gotten better on Dr. M's single medication. The cost difference between the antibiotic regimens was about a thousand dollars. It was certainly worth a thousand dollars to me not to have to experiment.

By the fourth day in the hospital, my white blood cell

count was barely elevated. I did not have a fever all day. I
was no longer pushing the button for opiate hits. I switched
to oral painkillers. It was April, and I went for a walk down
the long, polished, echoing halls of the hospital and out into
the bright sunshine. I sat down on a bench and felt its
warmth underneath me. A girl walked by eating an apple,
and I heard the crunch of her teeth and smelled the sweet
tangy scent of the apple. Victor was supposed to go to Peru
for a magazine photo shoot, and I said it was all right for
him to go. I would continue to recuperate at my parents'
house.

The next day I packed up the odds and ends that had ac-
crued in the hospital room in the course of a week: a half-
wilted pot of daffodils, a picture of my dog, a cheap CD
player and a stack of CDs, a toy dog with droopy eyes, the
overalls and sweatshirt I had arrived in, a few get-well cards,
a deflated balloon.

There was one minor mistake still to come: my home antibiotics did not arrive as scheduled. I waited on the porch for
the delivery man until half an hour before the next dose was
due. Spring sparkled around me, lacy pink azaleas and soft-
petaled dogwoods. There was a smell of freshly cut grass,
and peach blossoms, and the grainy smell of birdseed scattered by yellow finches. The sun felt warm on my face, and
I was thinking that I had to start living again. Illness sus-
pends time, but only for the one who is ill. Like Rip Van
Winkle, you wake up, and the seasons have changed; your
friends have children, and your parents, who have been sitting at your bedside, look older and tired.

The nurse arrived, but she did not have the medication. It
was to be delivered separately. We waited. My father pan-

icked. Who could blame him? Just five days before he had watched my head swell until it was as vast and precarious as the *Hindenburg.* He had watched me howl in pain. He had overheard doctors in the hallway discussing the possibility of a brain abscess or a transfer to the intensive care unit. He had heard strangers describe my immune deficiency as profound, grave, and life-threatening. We rushed back to the hospital, and I was given the scheduled dose of medicine in the outpatient infusion room, where the cancer patients go on weekends. When we returned, two sets of the same medication had been delivered. I could only laugh.

From then on, since I was in the care of my parents, things went smoothly. Things even went smoothly four weeks later, when I returned to the hospital to have the parotid gland removed by Dr. Grist. The surgical admission was routine. Parotids are removed for a number of problems, and although the ongoing inflammation in the gland might have made my surgery trickier than usual, it was nonetheless a protocol. The inflammation presented a challenge to Dr. Grist; it made all the tissues look alike, so that a nerve and a blood vessel and a ligament could blend together. Still, in his skilled hands the operation went well. The gland was removed before it became knotted in scar tissue, as the other gland had, and Dr. Grist was able to isolate and protect the facial nerve so that I do not have any nerve damage at all on that side of my face. I am now parotid-free. After eight miserable infections, I can never have another one.

I applaud all efforts to minimize medical errors, but medical mistakes come in different shapes and sizes. Some, like those committed by the first doctor I called, are the result of arrogance and laziness. These mistakes are unforgivable and should be punished. Others are the result of human fallibility. Wherever possible, there should be checks and rechecks to avoid these pitfalls, so that the wrong limb is never amputated, the right medication is always given, and the patient is treated as carefully and conscientiously as possible.

But sadly there will always be medical mistakes because, while medicine itself is an abstract and lofty concept, its reality is human: doctors, nurses, pharmacists, laboratory technicians, orderlies, and of course the patients themselves. And not only do we make mistakes, we work under a cloud of ignorance that is basic to the human condition. We are not omniscient. We are trapped in the present, and we cannot know the future or even all of the past.

In some ways, each illness reads like a murder mystery. A terrible event has occurred: the patient cannot breathe, the patient cannot walk, the patient cannot eat. These first symptoms are like finding the body floating face-down in the pool. Like detectives, the doctors work backward, but instead of thinking who might have wanted to kill Mr. Jones, we consider all the things that make a patient short of breath or nauseated or weak. These are our suspects. The illness progresses like an investigation; there are major and minor characters, and there are events that may seem insignificant at the time but turn out to have great import—for example, the fact that a patient has a slight headache. Similarly, there are events that seem to have tremendous significance at the time but turn out to be meaningless. We note that a patient has a history of exposure to tuberculosis. We will investigate this, just as the detective would investigate, say, a business partner who was cheated by the murder victim. But in the end, we find, it has no relevance to the case. The patient's difficulty breathing is caused by a tumor, not by tuberculosis.

When you finish reading a murder mystery, all the clues that led to the discovery of the culprit seem obvious, though they were often not at all apparent at the time. So too when a patient's illness has resolved—either in a cure or in death—the major facts of his disease seem obvious in retrospect; the clues that should have been explored immediately, chest X-rays or slightly abnormal lab values, the tests that should have been done—all seem abundantly clear, though at the time the doctor is working through a series of educated guesses, sifting through facts and theories, to find an answer. Each illness starts out as a mystery, and so it is inevitable that mistakes will be made as the mystery is solved. The wrong person is accused—it's the liver!—and then it turns out to be the lungs. The bullets from the suspected murder weapon do not match the bullets in the victim: the organism in the laboratory is not the one suspected in the patient. Such starts and stops are part of medicine, and though they may appear to be errors when the case is closed, the mysterious nature of disease means that some of them are inevitable and must be forgiven—hard as it is to accept this fact when the effects of the illness are felt on the body.

In my own case, the greater part of my injuries resulted from chance, bad luck, and wrong turns. I was lucky to live. Many patients have died from the same wrong turns. These deaths are tragedies, infinite and world-shattering to the people and families they affect. And they will continue to happen, every day, every year, as long as we are human.

The basic goal and dream of medicine is to strive for longer and better lives. To achieve that goal, we have developed sophisticated medications and instruments that seem nothing short of miraculous. It is easy to see how doctors can seem endowed with magical powers as we peer into the recesses of our patients' brains and hearts, as we bestow new organs on those with dying livers, lungs, and kidneys, and wave our wands to make infections and tumors disappear. But all the molecules and medications and instruments are delivered by human hands, and their use is limited by human knowledge and fallibility. The wizard behind the curtain is only a little man.

WHOM THE BULLET FINDS

love and death are the two great gifts that we pass on,
and usually they are passed on unopened.

——rilke, letters to a young poet

During my last year of medical school, my husband started taking pictures of my life, both as a patient and as a doctor in training. The first time he brought his camera to the infusion room, the head nurse, Charlotte, suggested patients whom she thought might be willing to have their pictures taken. She introduced us to a young man with a shaved head who spoke in whispers as his chemotherapy dripped into his veins. While he composed his face for a photograph, Patsy plopped down into the chair opposite us. She had on a plaid jacket and boots. She placed her hands on her knees in a matter-of-fact Annie Oakley style and declared, "You can take my picture." She wore wide round glasses that took up almost half her face and made her look like a cartoon character, a bug-eyed kid greeting the world. "In fact," she said, "you can even take it with and without my wig." She laughed and pulled off her wig to show a shiny head, as white as an eggshell, dusted with fine hair.

Patsy was getting a platelet transfusion. She'd been out of the hospital for a month after having had a bone marrow transplant for leukemia. Her transplant had not been easy. She'd developed a fungal infection in her blood and lungs; she'd been unable to breathe on her own for close to a month and had been in the intensive care unit on a ventilator. She'd also had a herpes infection in her throat, weeping sores on her legs, shaking chills, and high fevers. She related all this to me cheerfully as she posed for pictures. "I made it," she said. "I'm here now, and that's the only thing that matters."

A bone marrow biopsy done two days ago had shown no evidence of leukemia. There were no cancerous cells in her bloodstream. Patsy was thrilled. Her smile was so bright that it overcame her pale gray face, the shadows under her cheekbones, the large bruises on her arms and legs.

In the far corner of the room, next to the window, a young girl strained to hear our conversation. The nurse quietly whispered to Patsy that the girl, Jennifer, was scheduled for a bone marrow transplant herself, not for leukemia but for lymphoma, cancer of the lymph nodes. "She's terrified, poor thing."

Patsy swiveled her head around to study the girl. Like many of the patients in the infusion room, she wore a floppy hat to cover her bald head. Someone had given her the defiant pink button, also worn by many of the patients, that states flatly, "Cancer sucks." Three tentacles of a permanent catheter sprouted from her chest, and through one she was receiving an amber-colored liquid. Patsy was sitting on the stool with wheels that the nurses use when starting IV lines. She scooted over on her stool and stopped in front of the girl.

"Hi!" she declared.

The girl smiled politely.

"When's your transplant?"

"In two weeks," the girl said softly.

"Well, I'm not going to say it's easy," Patsy said. "It's not a walk in the park. But you'll get through it. You'll make it. Look at me." She twirled. "I'm living proof."

The girl smiled weakly. Patsy reached out and took her hand. She was quiet for a moment, and then she said earnestly, "You'll be fine. You will be."

One of the nurses brought out Patsy's platelets. She held up the frosty yellow bag, and Patsy went back to her assigned chair, opened the top button of her shirt, and pulled out her own permanent catheter.

"Once my platelets come back," she said to me, "I won't even have to come here anymore. I already don't need blood."

She pointed at my IV bag. "What are you getting?"

I explained that I had an immune deficiency and received antibodies every month. She was amazed we'd never met before, seeing as we were both regulars. Then, as if she'd forgotten, she giggled. "Of course, I've been in the hospital for the past three months."

Patsy watched as the nurse flushed her catheter and then hooked up the IV tubing. Charlotte told her that I was in medical school and then told me, "Patsy's a nurse."

Patsy nodded.

After three hours of sitting across from Patsy, I'd learned a lot about her. I knew she was a geriatric home care nurse, and that she preferred taking care of old people to babies because at least they could say thank you—some of them. She lived in a brick house in the suburbs and didn't like yard work. She had three stepdaughters, the youngest of whom was developmentally delayed. For fun, she and her husband went to Civil War reenactments. He was a Confederate soldier; she was a Confederate nurse. They traveled around the Southeast to participate in the anniversaries of various famous battles. For a time, she had worked at the Cyclorama, a gigantic circular mural depicting the Battle of Atlanta that was painted for a world's fair thirty years after the Civil War and remains a tourist attraction. She quit because the Yankees treated her as if she were defending slavery. "It's not defending slavery," she said. "Of course slavery was terrible, but we have a right to be proud of our history. Our boys fought hard."

She wanted to know where I was from, and she was pleased to learn I'd grown up in Atlanta. "There aren't many natives," she said.

I told her my parents were from New York, which explained the absence of a Southern accent. She smiled. "We'll forgive them," she winked.

She was full of questions. Had I enjoyed medical school? Parts of it, I said. I had not enjoyed getting up at 4 a.m. on my surgery rotations. I did not function well without sleep, and although I had mainlined Pop-Tarts and black coffee to try to stay awake, I had actually fallen asleep while holding the retractor during a particularly long operation. She looked at the magazine I was reading—*The New England Journal of Medicine*—and wanted to know if it was any good. I confessed that I carried it with me to infusions but rarely read much. I timed my infusions for the afternoon so I could watch my soap opera—something I wouldn't allow myself to do in any other circumstance.

Patsy could barely sit still while the platelets dripped into her body. She wheeled her IV pole around, visiting other patients and nurses in the room. She informed Victor that she wanted copies of the pictures he took. "I don't want to forget what I've been through," she said. "I'll use it to remind myself that things can always be worse."

I finished medical school three months after I met Patsy. I saw her once more in the infusion room. She was still feeling well, and she showed me pictures of her stepdaughters, little girls of five, seven, and nine years old, with dark hair and bangs, dressed for their portraits in identical red-and-green plaid dresses. "I'm not their real mother," she said. She looked at me. "I'm not their real mother, but I feel like I am, and I love them like they're my own." She looked at a picture. "That one," she pointed to the youngest, "especially needs me. That's why I couldn't die. I've got to raise these girls." She put the pictures away in her purse.

"Do you have any children?" she asked.

"Not yet," I said. "Just a big dog."

After that day, Patsy wasn't in the infusion room the times I happened to be there. I took that as a good sign—she might not even need platelet transfusions anymore. Perhaps her bone marrow was fully recovered.

I graduated from medical school, and then Victor and I took a belated honeymoon in Italy. When I came back, I started internship.

Internship is the first year of training as a doctor. After you graduate from four years of medical school, you are given the title "M.D." but you cannot legally practice on your own until you have completed an internship and a residency. Internship is a notoriously grueling year, with long hours—120-hour weeks are not unusual—sleepless nights, and intense pressure. For the first time, you are a doctor. You are allowed to make decisions on your patients without consulting anyone else. You can sign your name to an order on a chart, and the nurse will act on that order—give the medication, request the test, draw the laboratory value. In fact, the intern is overseen by a long chain of command: senior residents; fellows, who have completed their initial training, either in internal medicine or in surgery, and are now studying a subspecialty, such as hematology or cardiothoracic surgery; and, above the residents and the fellows, the attending physician, who is ultimately responsible for the patient. The intern can turn to any of her superiors for advice, but there is a general sense that seeking help is a last resort. You are left alone to sort out when to ask for help and when to muddle through on your own. On call nights, at 4 a.m., there is intense pressure to handle each crisis yourself rather than disturbing the slumber of the resident or fellow. No one expects the intern to sleep.

When I started medical school, I thought that I would be either a hematologist—a specialist in blood disorders—or an immunologist. Since the beginning of my medical training, I have loved hematology. Certain areas of study come naturally. Although my father is a cardiologist, I always found the heart baffling. I could not see the rhythms in the blips and lines of electrocardiograms; the telltale sounds a heart makes that reveal the underlying disease were always a mystery to me. On the other hand, the way blood works—red blood cells carrying oxygen, white blood cells fighting infections, platelets forming blood clots—always made perfect sense to me. I could study the workings of the bone marrow and the immune system for hours, whereas the workings of the kidney were guaranteed to put me to sleep. Part of this fascination, no doubt, stems from my personal interest. My medical problems are the result of malfunctioning white blood cells. The more I learn about these cells, the closer I feel to understanding what is happening to my own body, and the closer I feel to possibly finding a cure for my own disease.

As I went through medical school, however, I saw that it would be very difficult, given my health problems, to complete a residency in internal medicine—a prerequisite for an immunology or hematology fellowship. I ended up deciding on dermatology, a field that would give me a more manageable schedule but still involved elements of immunology and cancer. Before I could study dermatology, however, I had to complete a year-long internship.

I could have gone to an easier program, as my father begged me to; there are internships in private hospitals where call is every tenth night and often can be taken from the comfort of home. But I decided to stay at Emory, even though Emory's first year of medicine is a difficult one, with a tough schedule, little nursing assistance, and very difficult patients. I wanted to learn about bone marrow transplants and advanced cancers, and to do that, I needed to be at a major medical center. An internship at Emory also kept open the possibility of switching back to internal medicine if I found I had the desire and stamina. Since I was choosing a difficult internship, I also thought it best to stay near my family, in case I did get sick. Working at Emory, I would be up every fourth night, admitting and evaluating patients, performing spinal taps, putting in central lines, and checking EKGs. I knew I would run from floor to floor; I knew that much of the time I would be overwhelmed and exhausted.

As part of my internship, I had requested two months on the leukemia and bone marrow transplant units. Most interns do not want to do months on the leukemia service. The days are long, and the patients are complicated. In addition to cancer, they have problems with their hearts and lungs. They get infections; they have seizures; their kidneys fail. Their hold on life is fragile, and emergencies arise at all hours. Worst of all, most of them die. You find yourself becoming attached to patients in the very last days of their lives. Many of my colleagues find the frustration of losing patient after patient too great, and they would never choose to specialize in the field most often doomed to failure. They want to cure patients and send them on their way, remove the inflamed appendix, treat the infection, correct the heart's aberrant rhythm.

But it was the patients who drew me. In the infusion room in Atlanta, I sit in Bay 2, where the leukemia and lymphoma patients sit. Most of the patients I see and talk to during infusions are cancer patients. It's a generalization, but in many ways cancer patients are different from other patients. They are past all the petty squabbles of life, past worrying about new wrinkles on their faces or what kind of car they drive. They have been forced to the edge of life, where the important things come into focus: the love of their families, a sense of wonder at the world, an ability to cherish and feel time, like something solid you can hold in your hands, dirt or clay. I have found these patients uniquely open to their doctors; they tell wonderful stories. They carry pictures of their families, and the kindness that you can show them as a doctor—even when that is all you can offer—is received with gratitude. A doctor who feels that comfort is as important as cure will find hematology satisfying.

There was another reason for my request. Many doctors had predicted that someday I would develop lymphoma. I had learned about lymphoma in textbooks, but I wanted to see what it looked like firsthand.

I was diagnosed with cancer when I was twenty-one years old. When I was twenty-two, I was admitted to the hospital with sepsis. When I was twenty-three, I was again warned that I would most likely soon develop a terrible cancer. When I was twenty-six, I lay in a hospital bed in Aspen, Colorado, in so much pain I begged to be allowed to die. But I never actually thought I was going to die. I never felt my future crumble. Even when the doctor sat across his desk from me and told me straight out that I had cancer, I rejected the diagnosis instinctively. I never panicked; my heart did not quicken; my stomach did not sink. I could see over the doctor's shoulder to the gray sky and the gray filmy river. I looked at the diplomas on his wall. I shook my head. I was not numb or angry; I just knew I was right, and he was wrong. I was too young and healthy to be dying. I did not know at the time that there are many people who feel young and healthy and still have cancer. It would be much more difficult, now that I am a doctor myself, to reject this diagnosis. The process of accepting the real risk of developing lymphoma has paralleled the process of becoming a doctor.

The first time I truly felt I might die was in medical school. I was sitting in a small classroom, during my second year, and we were learning how to do the physical examination of the chest. The chief resident of the hospital explained the various techniques for assessing lung function. He then described the different heart murmurs and clicks

and gallops and what they might represent. Finally he reminded us of the importance of the supraclavicular lymph
nodes that lie just above the collarbone. Swollen lymph
nodes in other parts of the body may indicate viral or bacterial infection, even something as meaningless as a response
to a bug bite, but, he said, "if you can feel a supraclavicular
node, it always means cancer."

He pulled down the collar of his shirt and touched the
area where we would expect to find the node. Each of the
students reached up to feel the area on him or herself. Of
course, none of them found anything to feel—except me. I
had a very discernible swollen lymph node, about the size
of a Brazil nut. I felt my whole body flush, and I thought I
might be sick to my stomach. My head felt fuzzy, and the
room began to spin. I kept moving my hand away and then
back again, hoping I had been mistaken, but the small knot
remained. I did not tell anyone in the room what I was feeling. Class continued, and the chief resident went on to pass
out diagrams of the heart to study. His voice sounded as if it
were coming from another planet. I sat perfectly still, waiting for the hour to be over.

This time I did not reject my fears outright. I had spent
the last year and a half learning how the body works—and
how the body breaks down—and like all medical students, I
was at times overwhelmed by the body's fragility. This feeling is called "medical students' disease." It's commonly
joked that medical students convince themselves they have
each new disease they learn about: heart failure, Lyme disease, African sleeping sickness, Hodgkin's lymphoma, lupus.
During our lecture on melanoma, you could see all the medical students rolling up shirtsleeves and pants legs to examine their own moles. I never worried about these diseases.
I simply worried that the disease that had been predicted

for me—non-Hodgkin's lymphoma—had arrived. And this worry was reinforced by the discovery of that swollen lymph node on a Tuesday afternoon.

I called my immunologist the same day. She told me she was not surprised that I had a palpable supraclavicular node. In a sense, my immune system, unable to control the viruses that live in my body, strikes out desperately at everything else. My body is always fighting a blind and inefficient war, always mobilized but lacking the one weapon needed to kill the enemy. The swollen lymph nodes are the physical signs of this constant battle: in my chest, my pelvis, my legs, my throat. She was not concerned, she said, as long as I had no other symptoms to suggest cancer: no weight loss, no fevers or night sweats, no chills, no cough, no abdominal swelling or pain.

I was reassured at the time. And as a doctor, I have offered such reassurance to my patients hundreds of times, when it appears that we've caught their cancers early or when they are young and worried that a cough, which is most likely nothing more than bronchitis, means they have lung cancer. I don't offer the reassurance lightly; I do so when the statistics are grossly in my favor. The likelihood is 95 percent that a patient with an early melanoma will have a normal life span, and so I tell them not to worry, to go live their lives and not lose sleep. But as a patient, I know there is an immediate calculation: 95 percent is not 100 percent; some confidence is lost with each small blow to our bodies.

With each swollen lymph node, each abnormal biopsy, I am reminded that my body is fragile, more fragile than the bodies of other women my age. I never escape these abnormalities. Every Pap smear I have is suspicious for cancer. I don't see a regular gynecologist for my checkups, I go straight to the cancer specialist. Every new doctor who examines me is alarmed by the size of my lymph nodes and wants to stick a needle in one. Every new pathologist who examines what the needle draws out immediately thinks I have lymphoma. From time to time, new lymph nodes swell up, and from time to time, they go away. I get sore throats frequently, and I never know if they are going to turn out to be a devastating infection or just a mild cold. Swollen lymph tissue blocks my middle ears, so I have tiny tubes implanted in my eardrums to allow me to hear. Every six months or so the tubes fall out and leave me hard-of-hearing until I have them put back in. Lymphoid tissue has proliferated in my tear ducts, blocking the production of tears, and so I sleep with eyedrops by my bed to help me open my eyes in the morning. Every few weeks I wake up with my eyes burned red. They may look normal by lunchtime, or they may stay that way for days. So far these small erosions have only been inconvenient and annoying. My body has held its own, kept cancer at bay, and I have continued to live, even to live well. But I know that death—especially death from cancer— often starts from a tiny spark in the body, a twinge in the side, a little headache, a sudden need to nap in the middle of the day. And these small sparks grow, leap up in flames, to finally consume the body. Accepting the reality of this risk, I now realize, is part of the price I pay for being a doctor. It was much easier to reject before I understood the body's mechanics.

Now I do not fear death when I am acutely ill. Infections, I know, can be treated. My moments of anxiety come over small things, in the shower, when my hands run over my eternally swollen lymph nodes or I feel the scars of past surgeries. After I got married, I suddenly lost five pounds, without dieting. For most people I know, this would be a happy event. I was terrified that it signaled the onset of cancer. My various doctors all reassure me, and I take their reassurance, repeating it to myself when I wake up in the middle of the night. I tell myself that we all must live in the limited world of what we know because to try to live in the vast world of what we do not know would leave us groping in the dark, stumbling blindly and paralyzed with fear.

When I arrived on the sixth floor of the hospital, the leukemia floor, I found myself looking at the place where I might emerge after such blind struggling. I found myself, like Scrooge in *A Christmas Carol*, in a possible and terrible version of my future.

Internship year traditionally starts on the same day everywhere in the country: July 1. Those familiar with teaching hospitals often say it's bad luck to get sick in July, when the first doctor you will see was a medical student only one week ago. Emory starts a week earlier to squeeze in an extra seven days of vacation at the end of the year, so on June 23, I woke up at 5 a.m. to get to the sixth floor of the hospital by 6 a.m. I arrived with a newly printed ID badge that had the letters "M.D." after my name, a fresh white lab coat, pockets stuffed with books to help me with diagnoses and doses. I was the only doctor there. A list of patients had been left for me at the nurses' station, and I picked it up and gathered the corresponding charts to start familiarizing myself with medical histories. I had notecards in my pockets to write down the patients' names, medical record numbers, laboratory values, radiological studies, and important facts. I started filling them out.

Doctors break cancers down into two basic groups: the solid tumors and the liquid tumors. The solid tumors are those that arise in the body tissue itself, the brain, the pancreas, the intestines, the liver, the lung, the breast. These cancers, if caught early, can sometimes be cut out and cured. In fact, the chance for cure of early melanoma or colon or breast cancer is excellent. Other solid tumors are almost always incurable, often because there is no way to catch them until they have progressed. Very few patients survive cancer of the esophagus or the pancreas.

The liquid tumors, leukemias and lymphomas, are the cancers that arise from components of the blood. By definition, leukemia means that the cancerous cell can be found swimming in the bloodstream (*emia* means "in the blood"). In the case of lymphoma, the cancerous cell arises in a lymph node. The most common form of childhood leukemia, acute lymphoblastic leukemia, or ALL, is now usually cured. Some forms of adult leukemia can smolder along for years before suddenly becoming aggressive and fatal; others, like acute myelogenous leukemia, or AML, kill quickly without treatment but can be cured with a bone marrow transplant, particularly if the patient is young. Because the cancer cells are spread throughout the body, in lymph nodes or the bloodstream and bone marrow, there is no surgical cure for liquid tumors. There are two treatment options: chemotherapy alone or chemotherapy and radiation followed by a bone marrow transplant. I had studied the chemotherapeutic agents and had learned about bone marrow transplants in medical school, but I had never actually seen a patient enduring high-dose chemotherapy or radiation. I had never seen anyone undergoing a bone marrow transplant. I had memorized the terrible side effects of the medications—heart failure, seizures, kidney failure, vomiting, mouth erosions, bloody diarrhea, bloody urine, sterility—but I had never actually seen a patient accepting these poisons in the terrible bargain that cancer patients make in order to survive. Now I was to put names and faces to these facts.

Mr. C was first. From his chart I learned that he had recently left the intensive care unit; he had leukemia in his lungs and a fungal infection in his lungs, blood, and possibly his central nervous system; he was on seventeen different medications and required four liters of nasal canula oxygen. I went on to Mrs. S: chronic leukemia evolved into acute, has failed chemotherapy twice, here for salvage treatment, harbors an organism resistant to all known antibiotics in her gastrointestinal tract, must take contact precautions. Mr. W: eighteen years old, aggressive lymphoma, searching for a bone marrow donor, seizure disorder due to fungal infection in brain versus leukemia in brain versus chronic low magnesium secondary to damage done to kidneys by medication used to treat possible fungus in brain.

At six-thirty the resident arrived. He saw that I'd found my list and gave me my morning orders. Go around and see the patients, write down their last set of vital signs and most recent lab results, and ask how they are feeling, questioning especially their ability to breathe and to swallow and whether they are experiencing any fevers or chills, diarrhea or vomiting. Look in their mouths for sores and erosions, which could be caused by the chemotherapy drugs or infections, listen to their heart and lungs and abdomen, and examine them for rashes. All of this should take about ten to fifteen minutes per patient. Remember to wash your hands carefully before and after each patient—these patients have no immune systems, so any bug you bring into the room is likely to latch onto them. He said we would round with the attending physician in an hour.

I started out room to room, introducing myself as "Dr.

Weisman," a name that had always meant either my father or my grandfather. Mr. C was too weak to sit up in bed, so I couldn't listen to his lungs. His illness had started, as cancer often does, as a small problem. He had been on vacation in Williamsburg, Virginia, with his family when he came down with a cold. He couldn't shake the cold and felt more tired than he normally would with a virus, so he went to the emergency room. The doctors in the tiny Williamsburg emergency room drew some blood, and to their dismay—and Mr. C's—they diagnosed leukemia. He tried to shake my hand, but his arm was trembling too much. "Believe it or not," he said, "I'm a miracle man. They told my wife I should be dead." His face was ashen, and he had lost his hair in clumps so that a few strands of gray still clung here and there on his scalp. Next to his bed was a cup filled with saliva and blood.

Mr. W was, to my surprise, a chubby black boy who looked much younger than eighteen. Without his hair, he had an oversize baby face with chipmunk cheeks and bright eyes. His round face—it turned out—was the product of high-dose steroids, used to control his seizures, which ironically made him look healthier than he was. He did not smile at me. He felt like shit, he told me, and reluctantly sat up for his exam, opening his mouth and raising his hospital gown so I could press on his abdomen.

You want a patient's belly to be soft with no distinct lumps or bumps. I was examining these patients to see if I could feel the sharp edge of an enlarged liver or the sopping sponge of a fat spleen. Either one is bad news. When you press your stethoscope to the abdomen, you should hear the gurgle and whoosh of active bowels. Mr. W's abdomen was healthy and soft.

I had not finished seeing all the patients by seven-thirty,

but the resident found me and said we should get started on rounds anyway. Dr. Langston, the attending, had arrived. She was a young woman with a spontaneous, genuine laugh that seemed incongruous to her sad surroundings. She introduced herself and said, "Oh, first day of internship." She shook her head in empathy. "No one ever forgets their first day."

We sat at a conference table and discussed the patients along with a team of nurses, a pharmacist, and a social worker. The resident had already been taking care of these patients for three weeks. In fact, he would be leaving the service in a week, done with residency altogether and off to private practice. He knew the patients well, and he and Dr. Langston alternately smiled at those who were doing fine and had only mild complaints—Mr. M's hemorrhoids were still itching—and sighed over those who were getting worse. Some had failed all therapy and had no hope for a cure; for these we discussed, with the social worker, how to arrange hospice care that would allow them to die in the greatest possible comfort.

When we had run through the whole list, Dr. Langston stood up and said, "Let's go see them."

We walked from room to room. In the hallway on the oncology floor are several plaques that say, "In loving memory of . . ." There is also a bulletin board titled "Cancer Survivors," with pictures of the ones who made it: a woman in a wedding dress, a man standing on top of a snowy mountain, a woman on a horse, another woman next to a Christmas tree. There is a board with a Magic Marker for patients to record the number of times they've walked up and down the halls, and a map of the United States with pushpins marking their hometowns. Many of the patients stay in the hospital for weeks, even months at a time, and their rooms are decorated the way college students decorate their dorm rooms. As we walked from room to room, I saw pictures of family members, stuffed animals, get-well cards, and fake plants. (Real plants are not allowed in the rooms because they carry fungi and bacteria.) In one room, three angel dolls in glittery white dresses were suspended over the bed. In another there was a glowering poster of Beethoven. A young girl had a Tupac Shakur poster, and an older woman had a large portrait of herself, taken fifty years ago on her wedding day. Along the way, Dr. Langston pointed out the salient features of each patient's history.

"She has heart failure from daunorubicin."

"He's responded beautifully to the chemotherapy. Just a little tweak, and he's in remission."

We had almost reached the last room when Dr. Langston stopped. She sighed heavily. "How's Mrs. B?"

"A little better," the resident offered. "But she still can't eat."

Dr. Langston shook her head and looked at me. "This one's a sad case."

She pushed open the door, and we walked inside. A jungle of IV poles, bags of medication, and lines of clear plastic tubing obscured the bed. Dr. Langston pushed the lines aside to reveal heaps of sheets and blankets. A small head poked out from beneath the sheets. It was hairless, with yellow skin and wide eyes and glasses. I stepped forward. At first I was not sure it was Patsy, she was so changed, but I recognized her big eyes, and she recognized me. I wasn't sure whether to leave or stay; whether she would be happy to see me or angry or even embarrassed that her confidence had proved to be false. I flushed, embarrassed myself for some reason, perhaps at my own apparent health, the color in my face, fresh from a trip to Italy, the embarrassment of good fortune.

Patsy lifted a hand to wave at us, but it was clear that even this small movement caused her pain. She tried to speak but couldn't. The resident whispered to me, "Patsy's got herpes simplex esophagitis. It really hurts. She can't eat, so we're feeding her through a vein." He looked at my friend, little more than a rag doll tossed on the bed.

I didn't mention that I knew Patsy. I also did not say that I knew firsthand the pain of herpes esophagitis, how your throat feels shredded and trampled. I looked at Patsy and knew her fate could easily have been mine. During my two months on the leukemia and bone marrow transplant unit, I was to confront several patients with infections that I'd endured, patients who took the same medications I took, patients who shared the diagnosis I was predicted to develop. And while I tried to comfort and care for them, I also was forced to see a possible future for myself. I understood, as I never had known before, why my doctors looked so sad when they predicted I would develop lymphoma. I understood that they foresaw the awful torment of chemotherapy and radiation, the slender hope of a cure, the tragedy of an early death in a girl who sat on the examining table working through a crossword puzzle and blithely insisted that she was not sick and wanted to travel.

"She had a bone marrow transplant three months ago," the resident continued. "But her leukemia came back."

Dr. Langston asked Patsy how she was doing. She smiled weakly. In order to talk, she fished a bright green sponge on a plastic stick out of a Styrofoam cup of blue mouthwash and swabbed her blood-crusted lips.

"Better," she croaked.

I was standing behind Dr. Langston and the resident, but her eyes found me. She waved, and I waved back.

"I'm so sorry," I said.

The risks of any bone marrow transplant are high; the patient's immune system is temporarily destroyed in order to allow the new blood cells to find a home, not unlike razing an old house to put up a new one. During this time, the patient is an open target for any infection that might wander in the window. The common cold is a frequent killer of bone marrow transplant patients. The chemotherapy drugs used to destroy the immune system are toxic themselves. They can ruin a heart, a liver, or a pair of kidneys.

After the transplant, there is a whole new set of risks. If the patient has received bone marrow cells from another person, a family member or a stranger—a so-called MUD, or Matched Unrelated Donor—those cells will, at least to some degree, attack their new home, the body in which they have been implanted. Early in life, our immune systems learn how to tell friend from foe; in other words, they learn not to attack the body in which they live and to attack everything else that comes in. How exactly this recognition is learned is still a mystery, and a hot point of research. If we could teach the adult immune system to tolerate new things—a transplanted liver or bone marrow or kidneys—we could save thousands of lives.

When the transplanted bone marrow cells start to grow and attack the body that is their new home, a condition called graft-versus-host disease develops. For unknown reasons, the new cells attack certain body organs preferentially. Their first targets are the liver, the skin, and the gastrointestinal tract. The patient develops abdominal pain, diarrhea, rashes. She may progress to jaundice and liver failure. Over time her skin may turn so hard that she cannot bend her knees and elbows. A touch of graft-versus-host disease can be helpful because the cells may also attack any cancer cells that try to come back, but too much is deadly. Between a third and two-thirds of patients receiving bone marrow transplants from unrelated donors die of graft-versus-host disease instead of their original cancer.

Severe graft-versus-host disease almost never develops in patients receiving the third kind of bone marrow transplant: the autologous transplant. In this procedure, the patient is given back her own bone marrow cells—after they have been removed and purged to the greatest extent possible of any cancer cells. Because these cells are returned to their original home, they generally don't attack the body. But they also won't attack any remaining cancer cells. And since the retransplanted cells were the ones that turned into cancer cells in the first place, they may revert to their old bad ways and become cancerous again. The chance for relapse is highest with an autologous transplant.

After rounds, we sat down again to discuss the patients. No one in Patsy's family had matched her bone marrow, so she'd chosen an autologous transplant over a MUD transplant. She was one of the victims of its statistics.

In the past, some of my doctors had considered a bone marrow transplant as a possible cure for me. They had wanted to test my brothers to see if they could be donors. At Massachusetts General, the doctors had been on the brink of recommending at least a cycle of chemotherapy. As my immune deficiency was further defined, however, it became clear that a bone marrow transplant was not only unlikely to cure me, it would probably kill me. The viruses that I do not fight live in a tenuous equilibrium in my body. The immune system that I have, albeit faulty, has managed to keep them from triggering lymphoma or overwhelming my liver or my lungs. If we were to destroy that immune system—the necessary first step of any bone marrow transplant—the viruses would rage wildly. They would almost certainly kill me before a transplanted immune system could come to the rescue.

For Patsy, however, a bone marrow transplant had represented the best hope for a cure. And there was good reason to be optimistic. She was young, only thirty-seven, and before she developed leukemia, her organs had been strong. The doctors felt she could withstand the chemotherapy regimen. Patsy had done exceedingly well for a while. But leukemia is, in the words of Dr. Langston, "a bad actor," and it has a way of outsmarting the doctors and overwhelming its victims. It crouches behind brain cells and in the deepest recesses of the bone marrow, and just when you think you've swept it all away, it creeps out and floods the body once more. It was flooding Patsy.

After rounds I went back to visit Patsy. She was receiving three different antibiotics, an antiviral medication for her throat infection, painkillers, and nutrition, all through three giant tubes in her neck. She had clearly been in the hospital for some time. An angel figurine with a pink glittered skirt and a Styrofoam head sat on the windowsill. Drawings by her three children were taped floor to ceiling. A music box with carousel ponies on it sat next to her bed. I was at a loss for what to say. Two months ago both our lives had stretched before us. While we ate peanut butter crackers and sipped ginger ale and received the scraps of blood we needed to live, she'd talked of taking her children to Washington, D.C., to see the White House and the Capitol.

Patsy was not the first friend who had been walking beside me one moment, and the next seemed to have fallen off a cliff. There was MaryAnne from the infusion room in New York and Nora from the room in Atlanta, but both of them had already been sick and dying when I met them. Patsy, when I met her, was striding along as confidently as a majorette in a marching band. My sorrow for her was mixed with the awareness that I could be tripped as quickly and completely as she was. She was suffering from a painful infection that I knew firsthand, and while she had leukemia and I had been predicted to succumb to lymphoma, the end result would be the same. The blood cells die; the body is consumed with cancer, and you lie in a hospital bed, daily becoming more shadow and less human, until you take your last breath.

When the resident left the service, Patsy was assigned to be my patient. I was to see and evaluate her each day and report to the attending physician. It was also my responsibility to make sure she received whatever new medications or procedures the attending felt were necessary. If she needed a bone marrow biopsy or a spinal tap, it would be my responsibility to perform these procedures. I had gone from being her fellow patient to being her doctor in a matter of weeks, and Patsy accepted this change with grace. Every morning at 6 a.m. I went into her room to look into her mouth and listen to her heart and lungs. She cooperated with my examinations and even called me "doctor" once, although I told her to please call me Jamie. She was gradually improving, and she was desperate to leave the hospital. She and her husband had planned to participate in a reenactment of the Battle of Gettysburg on the Fourth of July. She had sewn new costumes, he had polished his sword, and they had plane tickets to Pennsylvania. Patsy had never been on a plane before. As a nurse, she knew that even if she were able to leave the hospital, she could not fly anywhere. She required daily transfusions and intravenous antibiotics. But, she told me, "I want to fly. I want to go on a trip before I die." July Fourth came and went, and she didn't leave the hospital. The plane tickets stayed in the bureau drawer.

Patsy's husband, mother, and mother-in-law were constantly in her room. They did not feel as obligated as Patsy did to smile for the doctors. Her husband, a heavyset man with dark hair and a face bruised blue-gray with sadness, sat slumped in a chair. He cared tenderly for his wife, holding a straw so she could take tiny sips of water, encircling her small hand in his large paws. He was always on the verge of tears. His three daughters bore an uncanny resemblance to him—all with deepset, dark half-moon eyes. I knew this from their pictures.

Patsy wanted to try again. She wanted another bone marrow transplant. She very clearly stated that she was not ready to die. But the first transplant had left her heart very weak, barely pumping. When her heart was fully evaluated, the doctors decided she could not withstand any more chemotherapy, that the treatment itself would kill her.

Patsy took the news that she could not receive another transplant with her customary stoicism. I wasn't with her when the attending doctor explained the situation to her. She passed the information on to me when I stopped by in the afternoon.

"No transplant," she said. "My heart's too weak. But"—she tried to brighten—"I get to go home."

The doctors arranged home health care for her, and Patsy packed up her room full of angels and artwork. She promised to see me in the infusion room. "Find out when I'm going to be there," she said, "so we can talk."

After Patsy went home, Dahlia arrived. She had been sent up from a small hospital in Savannah, because the doctors there were out of treatment options. Dahlia had a rare and aggressive form of lymphoma; it had persisted, unfazed, through three cycles of chemotherapy. When she arrived in the hospital, she was barely responsive because the disease had caused the calcium levels in her blood to rise to astronomical proportions. Excess calcium causes a number of problems, from kidney stones to constipation. It also affects the central nervous system and may cause the patient to appear confused or lethargic or even to slip into a coma. Dahlia's levels were so high that it was surprising she was not deeply comatose. In order to normalize her calcium, we had to pour fluids into her veins, and poor Dahlia could not sleep because she had to urinate every fifteen minutes.

When her calcium levels came down, Dahlia was able to talk. She had two children waiting at home in Savannah. I knew the area where they lived, a working-class neighborhood caught between the antebellum historic district on the waterfront and the post–Civil War renovated Victorian neighborhood. I could picture her home, a ramshackle two-story wood house with wraparound porches on the first and second floors. I'd seen these houses before, with laundry hanging from the railings to dry, the yards overflowing with the gray-green weeds that grow in sandy soil, bleached Big Wheels and rusted bicycles out front. Her husband worked at a gas station. Dahlia had been a housekeeper before she got sick. Her kids were seven and nine years old; they'd never been to Atlanta before. She wanted her kids to see Atlanta. Her husband was coming up to visit her, but she didn't want him to bring them. She didn't want them to see her so sick.

There was no good treatment for Dahlia's disease, but there was some evidence that high-dose interferon alpha—the same medicine I take—might buy her some time. It was not expected to cure her. Interferon has many toxic side effects. Almost everyone feels achy and weak from it, as if you're coming down with the flu. You get headaches; you may feel sick to your stomach, and you get depressed. Some people have more serious problems; they stop making blood cells, or their thyroid gland stops working, or their liver gets injured. Others get so depressed, they attempt suicide. We had to tell Dahlia about these possible effects before we started her on the medicine. She seemed scared at the prospect, even overwhelmed, so I broke my silence and told her that I had been taking interferon injections for nine years and was doing fine. I told her she would feel bad at first, but Tylenol and Advil would help, and she might even get used to the side effects and not need painkillers at all. I had.

I do not, as a rule, tell my patients about my medical condition. It always sounds self-serving to me, when they have their own problems to worry about. If I were a cancer survivor, I might share that experience with cancer patients, but I have such a rare condition that I have never had a patient whose diagnosis I share.

Dahlia looked at me incredulously. Unless you look closely, there are no signs of illness on me. You'd have to reach up and touch the swollen glands in my neck or turn my head around to see the scars from removing my parotid glands and various lymph node biopsies. "You take that medicine?" she asked.

I assured her that I did. She was going to be taking three times as much as I take, however, and she would probably feel much worse. I hadn't wanted her to be overwhelmed, but I didn't want to give her false reassurance either. I was concerned that she would think she could walk across the bridge of interferon to get to where I stood, when I knew that it was not going to be that simple.

"Do you have lymphoma?" she asked.

"No," I said.

She looked disappointed, then shrugged. "Well, I guess I'll give it a try."

Dahlia had her first shot of interferon that night. I had ordered it to be given at bedtime, along with some painkillers, because I had learned from experience that that would allow her to sleep through the worst aches and pains. She tolerated the medicine well, and when I saw her the next morning, she said, "It wasn't so bad. Now if only I could stop peeing." She was still receiving massive amounts of fluid, but her calcium had started rising again, and it was making her tired. She didn't want to get out of bed to walk. She barely agreed to sit up so I could examine her.

She was eventually given another course of chemotherapy along with her interferon, but her lymphoma thundered on. There was nothing to do for her. She had been given the maximum amount of chemotherapy she could receive without the medication itself killing her. Her husband came up from Savannah to take her home to die.

I walked into her room and found him sitting by her bed. He was a burly man with a faint mustache and the thick hands of a mechanic, with black oil etched into the palms and under the fingernails. He rose to shake my hand when I came into the room. He said, "Thank you for taking such good care of Dahlia."

I flushed. In reality I hadn't done anything for Dahlia except make her pee. She was no better off than when she arrived. I told him, "She's easy to like."

He glanced at the bed. Dahlia was dozing. "I guess we're going to go home now," he said.

I never saw Dahlia again. I heard from the attending physician that she died a few weeks after she left the hospital.

After Dahlia I encountered several more patients whose illnesses in some way intersected with mine, although all of them had developed cancer—my worst fear—while I still appeared perfectly healthy. One young man, Rob, had quit his law firm to go back to school and take premedical courses. In the middle of basic biology, he felt enlarged lymph nodes in his neck. He began to feel tired, and he was so sweaty at night, he would soak through his pajamas. He went to the public hospital because he had no insurance at the time; it had never occurred to him he could get sick. He was diagnosed with non-Hodgkin's lymphoma, the same disease I was always threatened with. He was only twenty-nine years old. While I cared for Rob, I did bone marrow biopsies and spinal taps, procedures I had endured myself. I never told him of my own experiences, but there are certain things I do when I perform these procedures that make them more tolerable, at least for me. I talk to the patient; I tell him exactly what I am going to do before I do it. I never let him forget that he is not alone. I encourage him to have someone else around to hold his hand. I tell him it's okay to scream and make noise. I know to do these things because I have screamed and talked and blathered through all my procedures. I remember one bone marrow biopsy where I recited, in increasing octaves, the birthdays of my friends, family members, and all the pets I had ever owned, including gerbils and turtles. Perhaps some patients prefer other approaches; I can only do for them what has helped me in the past.

Patients younger than I died. An eighteen-year-old boy crossed illegally into the country from Mexico seeking help for metastatic cancer. I had to tell him, through a translator, that nothing could be done for him, save comfort measures. I spoke, then waited as the meaning of what I had said hung in the air, waiting to be transformed for him, until finally he and his young pregnant wife wept. There was no reason for him to die and me to live. There is no reason for me to be ill and others to be healthy. Some people comfort themselves with religion and others respond with anger, but we all share in the same task, the most human task, of accepting our powerlessness. I have gone further than other doctors my age in this acceptance. My patients and their families have gone further still.

Patsy came back to the hospital two months after she left. I was working at a different hospital then. When I went for an infusion, the nurse told me that Patsy was back on the sixth floor and was not expected to live much longer. After the infusion, I went to see her. The blinds in her room were drawn; it could have been morning or night. Again, she was surrounded with IV poles. She was shrunken to a tiny string. A giant green plastic mask covered her face, and I could hear the hiss of oxygen. Her weak heart could not pump her blood forward. Instead, the blood fell backward, and her lungs filled with fluid so that it was difficult for oxygen to cross through the fluid to the blood that was, albeit slowly, trickling out to her body. She was receiving high levels of oxygen into her lungs to try to push more of the gas into her sluggish blood. Two monitors beeped symphonically, measuring her heart rate and her oxygen level, which remained low. Her husband was sitting in the shadows.

She lifted a hand to wave to me, and the tip of her finger glowed red where the oxygen monitor was attached. There was nothing I could say. I sat down next to her and asked if she was comfortable. She shrugged.

She removed her mask and, in a weak, rasping voice, asked how I was doing. I told her I was fine. "I'll bet you're working hard," she said. "You look tired."

In fact, I had been on call the night before and so had not slept for thirty hours. I tried to schedule my infusions for days after call because it gave me an excuse to get out of the hospital quickly, and I could nap while the medication dripped in. "I'm okay," I told her. I didn't tell her what she looked like. I asked her how her children were doing.

"They're all right," she said. She was quiet for a minute. The television was on overhead, and the audience of a talk show whooped about something. "Soon," she said, "I have to tell them that I'm dying."

"Will they be okay?" I asked, and immediately felt stupid. How could they be okay?

"I have to tell them," she said. "I have to say good-bye."

Patsy told me to go home and get some rest. I promised to come see her the next day. She said, "Take care of yourself."

Death is not pretty. In the movies, people lie in bed in lace nightgowns; their breath slows; they reach their hands out and, in a quiet sigh, they expire. I have seen many people die, and none have died like that. They rage. There is terrible pain and confusion. Their bodies bruise and bleed. They moan. After Patsy left the hospital during my first month of internship, a young man named Jesse was admitted for a possible bone marrow transplant. There was a large lump in the center of his forehead, like a unicorn's horn that had been sawed off. The lump turned out to be full of leukemia cells. Cancerous blood cells were flooding his brain, his skin, his bones, and his liver, and it would be impossible to save him with a transplant. Instead, Jesse stayed in the hospital to die.

Over the course of two days, his pain escalated, rising up from some deep source and persisting beyond the point where he could follow simple commands or even answer to his name. He required steadily increasing doses of morphine, to the point where he was receiving enough narcotics to kill a large animal, and he still appeared to be in agony. He moaned and writhed on his bed. His wife and his mother sat beside him, horrified at the sight. They begged for more morphine to quiet him. We switched to even stronger narcotics, but Jesse's body still bucked. It was impossible to know what he was feeling. He could not talk, whether because of the high doses of narcotics or the cancer filling his brain, or both. He breathed like a half-drowned man just pulled from icy waters, gasping for air, teeth chattering.

At one point, a nurse made the mistake of putting heart and oxygen monitors on Jesse. The machines started beeping wildly, indicating critical readings. The cacophony of whistles and bells seemed to mimic perfectly the frenzy of death. His panicked mother flew out of the room to get a doctor. The attending physician yanked the monitors' plugs out of the wall. "He's dying," she said. "We don't need machines to remind us of that."

When Jesse finally died, the nurse paged me to come officially pronounce him. I entered a room filled with weeping women: his mother, wife, and sister. The lump on his head was turning gray-blue from where blood was gathering and clotting. His lips were parted. He looked neither peaceful nor angry, just frozen. His mother kissed his hands.

He had died not more than five minutes before I arrived, but already his body was cool. His skin felt doughy and dry, and when I touched his neck to feel for a pulse, there was none of the warmth and flutter that we know, unconsciously, means life.

As an intern, I declared at least twenty deaths. The first few I remember distinctly, and then I lost count. Often I was called in the middle of the night to examine the bodies of patients I had never met. After all the struggle to remain alive, the machines, the ventilators, the surgeries, the medications, the act of declaring death is relatively simple. No one actually teaches it. You feel the neck for a carotid pulse, then listen for a heartbeat and breath sounds. The neck is cool and motionless; the chest silent and oddly thick and solid, like meat. Dead people seem to weigh more than the living, as if all the flutter of our bodies, our beating hearts and cascading blood, lifted us indiscernibly from the earth.

Then you turn to the family, if they are present, and nod. Often by the time we are called, the nurse has already assessed the situation, and the family knows the patient is dead. They need a doctor to fill out all the forms. Sometimes the patient is declared dead after an unsuccessful attempt at resuscitation, and then we are the first to break the news. You hug the family; you tell them you are sorry for their loss. Then you fill out the forms. You call a hotline for organ transplantation and answer a series of questions to see if any of the patient's organs might be used. If the patient has died of infection or carries a virus, like HIV or hepatitis, organs cannot be transplanted, but otherwise you are required to ask the family if they wish to donate any suitable organs. Even the very elderly and frail can often donate at least their corneas. You must ask the family what mortician they are going to use. Often you must ask them to consent to an autopsy. Then you fill out forms with names and addresses in triplicate, and sign your name and sign your name again. The family stays with the body for as long as they like. Then the orderlies come with a stretcher to take the body to a morgue. The body is covered in a white sheet and wheeled out of the room.

Confronted with mortality, every doctor thinks about his own death from time to time. We know that the same basic rituals will be followed for us. Some writers say that every death is unique, but I have found that every death is more or less the same. Every individual who dies is unique, but there are in fact only a limited number of ways for a body to stop functioning. The body narrows to the same common end point, and it is only a few crucial organs and a limited chemical balance that separate the living from the dead. The heart stops; the lungs are flooded; the liver disintegrates; and the brain, deprived of oxygen, stops firing the signals that command the body.

Sometimes this end point is reached quickly and painlessly. Trauma patients may hemorrhage and die quickly. A bullet to the brain or the heart can kill in seconds. A renal death, doctors often say, is a good one. The kidneys stop filtering; the patient's potassium rises; he has a heart arrhythmia and dies immediately. Other deaths are painful and long. Patients with heart failure grow weaker and weaker until they cannot maintain a high enough blood pressure to stand and walk. Gradually the heart fails to send blood to the brain. These patients die slowly but often painlessly.

Cancer deaths are never painless. Cancer cells fill the bones, pushing out against something that does not want to give way. The weakened bones shatter, and patients can neither lie in bed nor sit nor stand in any comfort. The cancer may invade the liver so that it cannot make the necessary proteins to clot the blood, and large bruises spill over the face and arms; blood leaks into the lungs and brain. Tumors compress the intestines and the throat so the patient cannot eat or swallow. Toward the end, the cancer may cross the heavily guarded blood-brain barrier, sneaking into the central nervous system to squeeze nerve endings or push against the brain, so the patient's breathing becomes irregular, gasping, and he may have seizures or tremors or delirium. He may cry out as if he has seen something monstrous, but he will not respond to his name; he will not recognize his loved ones, and there will be no way to know if, in fact, he has glimpsed something terrible or if these are just the sounds a dying body makes.

At 5 p.m., when call night starts, an intern's beeper springs to life. It goes off while you are in the middle of answering another call, and you start scribbling down the numbers, deciding which patient you have to go see first and which can wait. Residents page with last-minute instructions: Check a chest X-ray or look up the results of a lab. Make sure a patient gets his blood transfusion. Be aware that another patient might need to be transferred to the intensive care unit. The other interns and residents are leaving the hospital; you know you're in for a long night. You bolt to the cafeteria hoping there's time to eat something, but the beeper goes off while you're in line with your tray, then again when you sit down. You watch your food get cold. You're lucky if you eat half your dinner before someone has new onset chest pain or can't breathe, and you have to leave right away.

One night an attending paged me to advise me that one of his patients was probably going to die while I was on call. It is unusual for an intern, the lowest person on the totem pole, to be called directly by an attending. Usually the attending will tell the resident or intern working with him to make the phone call, but this was an important patient. The attending wanted to make sure things were handled appropriately.

I had been hearing about this patient, Mr. Sullivan. He had received a bone marrow transplant. The transplanted blood cells had refused to take root, and so he had been left utterly defenseless, kept alive with blood and platelet transfusions while various infections leached onto his body. Almost a month had passed, and it was clear that Mr. Sullivan's bone marrow was never going to recover. At some point, the transfusions would have to stop. But Mr. Sullivan's family refused to let him go. He was a young man, in his early forties, with two young children, a loving wife, a good career. He had everything to live for; he just wasn't going to get to live.

The attending had told me it was very important to get permission to perform an autopsy. No one knew why Mr. Sullivan's transplant had failed, and an autopsy might provide important clues. But the family had been flip-flopping on the issue, ready to consent one day, then refusing the next. I felt awkward about this request since I did not know the family at all, but it was my job as an intern to follow the orders of the attending.

Around 3 a.m. the nurse called to tell me that Mr. Sullivan had died. He had drowned in his own blood. He'd had a bacteria growing in his bloodstream that was untreatable by any known antibiotic. An experimental antibiotic was sent by a drug company, but it did not help. The infection caused Mr. Sullivan's liver to fail. He developed a condition called DIC, or disseminated intravascular coagulation, which caused blood clots to form all over his body, clogging the arteries in his brain, his lungs, and his kidneys. At the same time, he was bleeding internally and could not form blood clots where he was supposed to. He was hemorrhaging in his lungs, and that night, finally, his lungs filled with his own blood, so that no oxygen could pass through, and he drowned.

When I went to see him, his mouth was filled with congealed dark black blood. His eyes were wide open, a livid yellow. His wife was stroking his face and sobbing, wailing for him to come back and apologizing to him for something. At the foot of his bed were two photographs, one of a young boy, about ten years old, in a Little League uniform, and another of a girl, maybe eight, in soccer shorts with her foot braced on the ball. The pictures had been blown up onto cardboard and cut out in the shape of the children. They were propped up on easels, and they smiled down at their father, unaware that he had died. The nurse told me later that he had requested these pictures so that he could see his children every day, although he could not bear the thought of them watching him disintegrate.

Hypochondriacs may love to fantasize about their loved ones weeping around the gravesite, but those of us who have had to seriously think about our own deaths are not comforted by this image. It is agony. It is the worst part of mortality. Worse than the cities you won't visit, the books you won't write; worse than not seeing your children grow up or not growing old with your husband; worse than all these things is the thought that the people you love will suffer, that they will be lonely and grieve. I fear sometimes that my father would not know another moment of joy if I died. I fear that my husband would never be able to love again. Mr. Sullivan, I am sure, had the same fears, for the pain that his family would feel, that he could not stop—could probably only sharpen—by loving them.

I turned to Mr. Sullivan's mother and told her I was sorry. She nodded. Then I asked if the family would consent to the autopsy. She touched her daughter-in-law's shoulder lightly. "They want to do an autopsy," she whispered.

The woman raised her tear-streaked face to me. She blinked. I said, "It would give us important information. Maybe someday it would help us save another patient's life."

The woman rubbed her eyes. She asked, "Will he be cut to pieces?"

I told her she would not be able to tell the autopsy had been performed. The children smiled at us with white, white teeth. It might save their lives. "Okay," she whispered.

Not all of the patients I cared for on the hematology/bone marrow transplant wards died. Mr. C, the patient I met on the very first day who shakily assured me that he was a miracle man, did in fact live. I ran into him in the infusion room a few weeks after he had been discharged. Again, I had been up all night on call. I was wearing my dark blue scrubs—had been in them, in fact, for more than twenty-four hours. My eyes were red, and my lips were chapped; they were always chapped after call. I had settled into my chair; the nurse brought me a blanket, and I was ready for a nap when I saw him across the room. I trundled over to say hello, carrying my IV pole with me.

Mr. C was so accustomed to seeing me as his doctor that he did not register the fact that I had an IV in my arm. He assumed I had come to check on him, and he started updating me on his condition. He told me he was receiving intravenous blood and medication to treat a fungal infection. He had just completed a second course of chemotherapy and was considered in remission. Remission means there is no sign of cancer at a particular moment; it does not mean the patient is cured. When I met Patsy, she was in remission. Depending on the cancer, a patient must go five or even ten years without showing evidence of cancer before a doctor will venture to call her cured. Still, Mr. C was pleased to have at least reached remission, meaning he could go forward with a bone marrow transplant. A match had been found. He was still weak, occasionally dizzy, and he needed a walker, but he could get to the kitchen to get himself a glass of water. He gestured to his wife and said, "She doesn't have to wait on me hand and foot anymore." Then he looked at me and asked, "Are you working over here now?"

His wife said, "Honey, she's got an IV in."

His eyes shifted from my face to my arm and then up the clear plastic tubing to the bag of fluid.

"What happened?" he asked.

"Oh," I told him, "I come here every month. I have an immune deficiency. I don't make antibodies, so I have to come here and get them. It's kind of like getting a blood transfusion."

"Do you have cancer?" he asked.

"No," I said.

"Well, I'll be." He stared at my arm where the needle disappeared into a vein.

Mr. C went on to get his bone marrow transplant, and the last I heard, he was at home, not in perfect health, but improving every day.

Patsy died in the hospital. I saw her a week before her death. When I came to the sixth floor, there were three little dark-haired girls in the waiting room. One of them was crying. I recognized them from their pictures, but I could not remember their names.

In her room, Patsy was smaller than ever. Her skin was almost translucent, and her head teetered on her neck like an egg on a stick. Her glasses masked almost her entire face. Most of the IV lines had been removed. She was receiving medication to make her comfortable, to control her pain and nausea, and to keep her from crying out when she dozed off. She wore a pink satin dressing gown that spread over her bed like water. I stood by her bed and told her I'd seen her daughters. I said they were very pretty.

"I told them," she said. "I said good-bye." I could barely hear her over the whoosh of oxygen. Her voice was gravelly and faint.

"How did they take it?"

She blinked slowly. "I don't think the youngest one understands. The oldest one cried. I'm worried about the middle one. She didn't say anything."

"I'm sure they know how much you love them," I said, but we both knew that that fact didn't change anything. The love of a dead person is abstractly comforting, like great poetry and music, but it is nothing compared to touch. In a few days' time, Patsy would touch her children for the last time.

Victor knocked on the door. He had been on the floor taking pictures of other patients and stopped in to see Patsy. She saw his camera in his hands, and just as she had done the day we met, she offered, "You can take my picture, if you want." Victor looked at me for permission.

"Are you sure?" I asked. She nodded and shrugged.

Victor lifted the camera. Patsy stared frankly into the lens, and the shutter clicked.

Patsy's mother told us that Patsy seemed tired and asked if I could stop by later. I said I would. We turned to leave, and Patsy whispered to Victor, "Take care of Jamie."

The next day I was on call and could not leave the hospital where I was working. I stopped by Patsy's hospital the day after that, and after looking up some lab values on a patient of mine, I pulled up Patsy's labs. I saw that none had been drawn that day, and that was how I knew she had died. When I went to the floor, her room was empty. The angels and the drawings and the music box, the scrap of a woman with enormous eyes, the Confederate nurse, the mother, all of it was gone. A neatly made bed, perfectly flat with a pink blanket tucked in, stood alone in the middle of the room. Another person would come to this room soon, another fight for life.

I've often wondered if Patsy thought—as I thought—that it could have been me lying in the hospital bed and her at the bedside, offering faint consolation. I wondered if any Faustian bargains had flashed through her mind. Why shouldn't we trade places? She had three children who depended on her. At the time, I had none. She had lived a modest, good life, gone to church, and asked for few rewards, and life had responded with this terrible injustice.

Did my daily visits remind her of that—more so, in a way, than the visits of other people who had not stood at the edge of the abyss with her? After all, Patsy and I had been to war together. It did not seem odd that those who stayed behind should live; they had never left the safety of their bedrooms. What seemed odd and unfair—to me, and I suspect to her—was that the bullet had found her and not me.

I have searched for meaning in mortality. This, I suppose, is the great question of human existence, the question that has puzzled philosophers and prophets through the ages, and I am certainly no more likely than Aristotle or Maimonides to come up with an answer. After all the death I have both seen and feared, I can't find any real meaning in it. Perhaps my own awareness of the fragility of life has increased my appreciation for it, but I can be as petty and jealous as anyone. I get annoyed with my patients. I am selfish and sometimes self-pitying. Good people and bad people die, and the world absorbs their losses alike, the way after a few waves the ocean fills a hole dug at water's edge. It fills the space that Patsy and Jesse and Dahlia and Mr. Sullivan left. It will fill the space I leave too, and a nagging, elusive pain, somewhere in the minds of the handful of people who loved me, is all that will last.

BEGOTTEN

*a father's no shield
for his child.*

——robert lowell, "fall 1961"

A twenty-three-year-old woman in a gingham shirt and blue pedal pushers waits with her three-year-old son in an obstetrician's office. She sits on the examining table, swinging her legs. The woman is eight months pregnant, and she is puzzled by how much weight she has gained. She is only five feet tall, and her belly is huge, tipping her forward. She can barely eat; all night she lies awake watching her stomach squirm. It's as if she's got eels or snakes or rabbits in there. Sometimes it scares her. During the day, she walks with her hands on her hips and sways like a tree. She's too tired to do anything; she hasn't cleaned the house in weeks. She can't concentrate on a book. She just lies on her side and stares out the window. Her son is sitting on the floor with his crayons and paper. There is no one to leave the child with, so he is her constant companion. Her husband has dragged her out to Salt Lake City, far from Manhattan, where her parents live.

The doctor walks into the room. He is also a displaced New Yorker, Dr. Kaiser from Brooklyn. He has been out of town and hasn't seen her for a few weeks. He takes one look at her and says, "That looks like twins."

He presses his cold stethoscope to her stomach; then he goes to get a colleague. The woman cannot see over her abdomen to monitor her son, but she hears the sound of running water. She looks up at the ceiling where the tiles meet. She calls to her child to stop playing with the faucets. The room is very quiet. The two doctors return. They bend over her belly, stethoscopes sprouting from their foreheads. Out of the corner of her eye, the woman sees her little boy putting something into his mouth. "What's he eating?" she cries.

Dr. Kaiser glances to the side. "Vaginal jelly," he says calmly. "Perfectly digestible." The doctors stand up straight and look at each other. Dr. Kaiser tells my mother, "There are two heartbeats. One at 140 and another at 160 beats per minute."

This information means nothing to my mother. The doctor points at her stomach. "Two heartbeats," he repeats. "You're having twins." He is smiling as if this were wonderful news. There are two lives floating in the warm pulsing fluid of her belly.

"Oh, my God." My mother is in shock. She pulls her shirt down and her pants up and grabs my older brother. She runs and waddles through the hospital over to my father's office. My father is twenty-six. He has finished his internal medicine residency and is now serving time in the public health service in lieu of joining the army. In a year, he is supposed to start a cardiology fellowship at the grand sum of two hundred dollars a month. He is talking to a nurse when he sees my mother walk in. She waves to catch his attention, and she holds up two fingers, as if she were making a peace sign.

"Two centimeters dilated." He smiles. He has predicted she is further along than eight months, given her size.

She shakes her head. "No, two babies."

My father drops the chart he is holding. He has to grab the countertop to steady himself. Then he decides he does not believe her. "You've got to be wrong," he says. "It's impossible. There aren't any twins in the family. We can't have twins. We can't. We can't afford it. What are we going to do?" My father leaves his patients and goes to see the obstetrician himself. He says there must be a mistake. "We can't have twins," he tells the doctor. "We just can't. You must be wrong."

The obstetrician is the head of obstetrics at the University of Utah. He has delivered thousands of babies. He tells my father he is certain my mother is carrying twins. He says, "I am never wrong." My mother climbs back onto the examining table, and the doctor finds the heartbeats again, distant frantic trills, like a pair of butterflies caught in a net. He hands the ears of the stethoscope to my father. "Listen," he says.

My father listens but still shakes his head. "It's impossible," he says. It was going to be tough to make ends meet with one child, harder still with two, but three! His mind ticks ahead to picture his family starving in a slum, the children with scabbed knees, crying in hunger. The wind blows through the house. They can't afford heat or hot water. The children have runny noses. "There are no twins in the family," he repeats. Then he demands, "I want an X-ray."

The doctor considers his request. My mother is past the point at which an X-ray can damage the babies, so he agrees. He shrugs. "You'll see."

In another room, my mother hoists herself up onto a cold metal table and lies flat. The room darkens, and a voice tells her to hold her breath. Then a light flashes over her. A few minutes later she stands with my father and the doctor, looking at a gray X-ray that shows two babies in her womb, curled heads down, almost kissing. My father cannot speak. He presses his hand to the picture as if he can feel us.

"What am I going to do?" he asks in despair.

The obstetrician takes down the film. He looks at my father and says, "Buy another crib."

Three weeks later, ten days before her due date, my mother and father have invited people over for brunch. My father has recently returned from a conference in Miami with delicacies unheard of in Salt Lake City in 1965: bagels, lox, and cream cheese. My mother is now gigantic. She lies in bed and compares her stomach to the mountains they can see outside the window. She can barely breathe. She cannot eat at all. She has to pee every five minutes. When she isn't peeing, she's burping. There is no room in her body for anything. Two days ago my older brother wandered down a ravine, and she had to gather up neighbors to rescue him because she knew if she went down, she'd never get back out. She is ready to have these babies, even if my father isn't.

My father sets out the bagels on a platter. My mother has

been feeling pressure all morning. She tries to go to the bathroom, but she can't. She just feels a watermelon sinking down on her hips. She tells my father, "Something doesn't feel right." She doesn't feel contractions, exactly, just a heaviness. It's different from how it felt with my older brother. She tries to ignore the feeling. The lox looks beautiful, pink and fresh on the plate. She can't imagine eating it.

"I'd better call the doctor," she tells my father.

The doctor tells her to come in right away. He tells her she is probably in labor.

"But it doesn't hurt," she says.

"It doesn't have to hurt," he tells her.

"Evan," she says, "we have to go to the hospital."

"Now?" he asks through a full mouth. He is already eating a bagel.

"Yes. Now!" People are supposed to be arriving any minute. My parents leave anyway.

By the time they get to the hospital, my mother is fully dilated and effaced. There isn't time for anything; no epidural, no painkillers. Dr. Kaiser walks in, calm as always, smiling. He touches my mother's forehead. "Are we ready to have these babies?" he asks. She has prayed that he will be in town to deliver her. She doesn't trust anyone else. He pulls on a glove, and she feels his hand inside her. "They're coming," he says.

"Is it time to push?" my mother asks.

"Almost," the doctor tells her.

Nurses are buzzing around the room. Dr. Kaiser says, "We're going to have a baby any minute now. Get set up." He puts on a blue gown. He winks at my mother and tells her, "I'm going to send a resident in here to examine you. Don't tell him you're having twins. I want to see if he can figure it out."

My mother nods mutely, although she is thinking to herself that this is no time to be playing games. My father has gone to take my older brother to the Katzes' house. He said he'd be back in five minutes. She's sure more than five minutes have passed. Her legs are in the stirrups.

The resident comes in. He tells her, "I'm told there's something special about you." He snaps on gloves and reaches in to examine her. My mother feels as if her vagina is Grand Central Station. "You're having twins, right?" he says. He's grinning, proud of himself.

"Yes, yes, you win the prize," my mother says. "Where's Dr. Kaiser?" Her body tightens with a contraction. She winces. "Where's Dr. Kaiser?" She is yelling now.

Dr. Kaiser comes bustling back in. My father is trailing behind him. The doctor sits between my mother's legs. My father holds my mother's hand. "I'm going to push now," my mother says. She is strangely calm. She thinks she ought to be in more pain, but she's not. The nurse stands behind the doctor. There is a tray of instruments, silver forceps and scissors and things my mother hopes they won't have to use, something that looks like a gas mask, a scalpel.

"I can see the baby's head," Dr. Kaiser says.

My mother is panting. My father is telling her she's doing a good job. She feels like a puppy. She pushes again. My brother Jonathan's head appears. My mother lifts up to see, but he's entirely wrapped in the doctor's big gloved hands.

"Here come the shoulders," Dr. Kaiser says. The baby slips out with a splash.

Jonathan's head has been molded by the birth canal, so he's got a triangular forehead like a mountain peak with a thick crop of black hair on top. "You have a baby boy," the doctor beams. Jonathan stares, unblinking, at the world he has just entered. The doctor clamps the umbilical cord and cuts. He hands the baby off to a nurse.

"We're not done yet," the doctor reminds my mother, as if somehow she might have forgotten. Then labor stops. She feels nothing. She could be walking on the beach or eating breakfast. There are no contractions; the pressure is gone. She could sit up and go home. But she knows there's another baby in there. She panics. She has heard stories of second twins born a week after the first. Dr. Kaiser's record is *six* weeks between twins. "Make it come out," she pleads.

They give her a shot of pitocin, and finally, swimming like Esther Williams down the birth canal, I emerge, with a perfectly round head, not a hair in sight, and eyes wide and livid. I scream the moment I see the bright lights.

"You have a little girl," the obstetrician declares. "And she's perfect."

He shows me to my father. A little girl at last.

My father grew up the oldest of three boys. He has never been around dresses and dolls, tea parties and dance recitals. A little girl is as exotic and wonderful as Paris or a trip to the moon, as terrifying and unknown as the bottom of the ocean or another galaxy.

Three days later my mother's parents fly out to visit. My grandfather had a daughter and a son. He stands with my father in the nursery where there are, in fact, two cribs, one with a blue blanket and one with a pink blanket, one with a blue dog and one with a pink dog, one with a boy baby and one with a girl baby. My grandfather picks up my brother and admires him. Jonathan has spiky hair and black marble eyes and a gurgly laugh. He picks me up, and it is like picking up his own daughter again, only now that daughter is a mother, a mother who has brought three new lives into the world, including the one he holds in his hands. Not so long ago she stood in his living room and showed him the ballet positions she had learned. First position, second position. She moved her tiny feet on the Oriental rug and held her arms carefully to the side. Not so long ago she woke up early in the morning and stood next to him while he made pancakes, and then they snuck out to the park and she showed him how fast she could pedal her tricycle. I am wearing a white shirt with a satin ribbon. I still don't have any hair. My grandfather tells my father, "You're going to have fun with this one."

My father tells him, "I don't think I'll love them any differently."

"Oh, yes you will," my grandfather says. "You'll see. A daughter is different."

He hands me to my father, and my father holds me.

We have been over to other people's house for dinner, and we are returning home late. I am lying down in the far backseat of the station wagon, drowsy, watching the streetlights bob into view and then bob away. Jonathan is asleep on the seat across from me. Mark is in the middle row of seats, and my parents are up front, talking in murmurs. I can't make out what they're saying. We are almost home. I close my eyes and pretend to be asleep. This is a trick I have learned. If I am asleep, my father will carry me upstairs.

I know when we pull into our driveway because it's a little uneven at the edge, and I can feel the car bump. I keep my eyes shut and do not open them even when the bright lights of the carport shine in. I hear the car doors open. I hear Jonathan wake up and stretch. The car pings until my father takes the keys out of the ignition. My mother comes around and opens the back of the station wagon, and I hear Jonathan jump out. I am careful not to move. My mother says, "She's asleep." My father reaches into the backseat and gently pulls me out. It's easy for him to carry me. He doesn't make a sound when he picks me up. His shirt smells like fresh laundry, and under that is a salty smell, a little like the dog but better. I hear the screen door swing open and feel myself carried through the living room and upstairs into my bedroom. This is the best feeling in the world, the safest feeling. Nothing can get to me as long as my father is holding me, not the thing in the closet I sometimes see where my grandmother's old caftan hangs, not things that might be under the bed or that scratch at the window. Superman himself could not make me safer.

My father doesn't turn on the light in my room. He lays me down on the bed and pushes the stuffed animals aside. I have thirty-three stuffed animals, seven of them koala bears. My father pushes down the sheets to tuck me in. He slips his hands out from underneath me, then pulls the sheets and comforter up to my neck. He tucks me in so the sheets are snug around me, and he kisses my forehead. He tiptoes out of the room and twists the handle of the door so it won't even click when it closes. After he is gone, I squirm because there is too much love in me to stay still.

I am eating a strawberry ice cream cone, using the bright pink plastic spoon I saved after sampling three other flavors. At my request, my father has taken us to Baskin-Robbins. My brothers told me to ask him if we could go, knowing he almost never says no to me. At Baskin-Robbins, I always sample three flavors, and then I get strawberry. I am tempted by bubble gum because when you are done, you still have the pieces of gum left to chew on, but it isn't as good as strawberry. My brothers devour their ice cream. They will be left panting as I slowly, methodically work my way through the second half of the cone, licking as delicately as a cat. I relish that moment.

The fluorescent lights are bright in the ice-cream parlor, and we sit at tables that look like school desks. The light bounces off the glass shields under which the ice cream hums, beautiful barrels of pink and white and yellow. There is a suggestion box for new flavors, and my father picks up a form. He looks at me while I work my way through the ice cream. He pretends to be thinking very hard, and then he says, "How about sauerkraut and fudge?"

"You suggested that last time!" I tell him.

"Lima bean and mocha?"

"Oooh." I make a face and giggle. He carefully writes it down and folds it into the suggestion box.

These are the things only my father can do for me: throw me in the air in the swimming pool, pitch a softball so slow it practically lands on my bat, come up with a dozen nicknames, all variations on Pipper Papuffnickle, tell me outlandish stories with such a straight face that I believe him every time. I am so gullible that he finally gives me another nickname: "Really?" My father teaches me to play a special kind of poker where you hold one card up to your forehead so everyone else can see it. We bet with toothpicks. He nicknames me "Poker Face," and I don't realize until much later that this is a joke because when I have a good hand, I jump up and down in my seat. He puts me on his shoulders and trots through the house so I can slap the tops of doorways. At the Macy's Thanksgiving Day Parade, I watch from my father's shoulders, feeling gigantic, even though our combined height is probably not much more than six feet.

When we go skiing, my father sits at the feet of each of his three children and is the only one strong enough to pull tight the buckles on our boots.

My father carries the movie camera. He does not understand that unlike with a regular camera, when you turn the movie camera sideways, you don't get a taller picture. Instead, everyone stands on their sides, defying gravity. There are movies of us waving in the shallow waves of the Atlantic Ocean, and then suddenly the world spins and the ocean and the waves rise up vertically and my brothers and I stand as if our feet are stuck to the wall, and the sky spills down sideways. My father takes the camera with him to film horse-back-riding competitions, soccer matches, go-cart rides, and birthday parties, and in all of them, there are moments when the world turns sideways.

I love to read, and every week my father takes me to the local bookstore, Ardmore Books, where a man with thick glasses and a five o'clock shadow helps me pick out new books. His name is Mike Ardmore, and his father, a short man with white hair and a big belly, owns the store. I read books about Indian girls and a boy in the Revolutionary War; I read *A Cricket in Times Square* and *The Yearling* and *Harriet the Spy* and *To Kill a Mockingbird*. I start reading as soon as we sit down in the car. My father laughs because sometimes I have already finished the first three chapters by the time we are home. I love the smell of the books, and the way the paper feels and the gloss of their covers. I line them up on the shelves in my room. In the summer, I can ride my bicycle to the bookstore and buy any book I want. My father stops off after work and pays the bill.

My father always makes me laugh, and he laughs at me.

He is scared of roller coasters. When we go to Disney World, he rides the Mad Tea Cups and "It's a Small World," but my mother goes with us on the roller coasters. One year we convince him to go on Space Mountain. We get strapped into the car, with me sitting in front. I am not at all scared. I can even hold my hands up in the air through the whole ride. As we are pulling out, there is a sign that reads, "People with heart conditions or bad backs and pregnant women should not ride this ride." My father yells out, "I'm a pregnant woman!" But they don't let him off.

It's the middle of summer, and we drive up to Lake Lanier Islands for the day. I am sitting in the middle of the backseat of my father's olive-green Dodge Dart with my brothers on either side. I have tucked a towel under my legs so I do not come into direct contact with the doggy throw-up stain on the car upholstery. My brother Jonathan is calling out the words for a Mad Lib. He asks for an adjective, and my older brother offers "conceited." I don't know what that means, but it's something he calls me a lot. I know it isn't nice. Then he asks for a noun, and I say "toilet." In the front seat, I hear my mother exclaim, "Really!" Jonathan snickers when he writes it down.

I am eight years old and wearing a yellow one-piece bathing suit with a cut-out in the middle in the shape of a daisy. It belonged to someone else before it was mine, but I still think I look great in it. I'm hoping to get a tan on my stomach in the shape of the flower. My flip-flops are already giving me a blister between the first and second toes.

When we get to the lake, my father unloads the car. We walk down a shady path littered with pine needles to the lake. There is a beach of fake sand that I know isn't like the sand in Florida. This sand gets squishy in your hand, like clay. On the way, we pass a concession stand selling Slurpees, and I make a note to ask my father for one later, a cherry one. Two boys are standing by the stand with their shirts off, and you can see the line of whiter skin around their waists where their bathing suits are pulled down an inch. We reach the beach. It's crowded, but we find a place to spread a blanket. My mother takes out a book and lies back. My brothers and I head down to the water's edge. I dip a toe in carefully. My older brother wades directly out.

A lifeguard in red shorts watches a swimming area marked off with a string of red, white, and blue floats. Beyond the swimming area, there are sailboats and paddle boats. To one side is the dock where you can rent the boats. I see Jonathan looking at the boats. He is a good sailor. He sees some people paddling a red kayak. He points it out to me. "I want to do that," he says. He dives into the water to get wet, then trots back to my father.

My father walks with him over to the dock. I tag along. My father rents him a kayak. It's red and smells like a new car. Jonathan zips on an orange life vest and reaches up for the paddle. A teenage boy takes my father's money, hands Jonathan the paddle, and unties the boat. He pushes the kayak off in the right direction. The water ripples. Off the dock, tiny fish flit around the poles. Jonathan paddles off, far out into the lake, until he is just a red blip. When he finishes his hour on the lake with the kayak, he tells me it was great; he went almost all the way across the lake, out to where the sailboats are.

My father asks me if I want to try. Jonathan tells me it's easy. I shrug. "Okay," I say.

My father puts his hand on my shoulder and says to the teenage boy renting boats, "We have another brave kayaker for you."

The boy doesn't say anything. He picks up an orange life jacket and hands it to me. It smells like mildew and sand, and I turn it inside out before I put it on. The boy tells me it's too big for me and gets me a smaller one. My father buckles the life jacket in place and checks to make sure it won't slip over my head. The teenage boy steadies the kayak for me while I lower myself in. He shows me how to hold the paddle. He has sandy blond hair and a wisp of a mustache, and his breath smells like grape bubble gum. He tells me to go anywhere I want except for the swimming area. Then he gives me a push away from the dock, and the water swirls behind me.

I start paddling. It is not as easy as Jonathan made it look. The paddle is heavy, and it lands in the water with a splash. I have to use all my strength to make the boat go forward, and then it doesn't want to go in a straight line. I bump right back into the side of the dock; the boy pushes me away with his foot. I wield the paddle like a sword, slamming it into the water and pulling the boat out into the lake. It's going in circles. Finally I advance about ten feet. I twist around to wave to my father triumphantly. I am on my way. Then the kayak decides it doesn't want to go where I tell it to. It wants to go to the right, to the roped-off swimming area. I thrash at the water with the paddle, to no avail. The boat has a mind of its own. It wants to go into the swimming area. It is pulling me there like a dog on a leash, and I am powerless. This cannot be the same boat my brother effortlessly guided out to the lake. This boat is broken! This boat is evil! This boat is taking me to forbidden lands! I swat at the red and white buoys on the rope that marks off the swimming area, but that only pulls me closer. On the shore, the lifeguard whistles at me and waves his hands away, as if I didn't already know I wasn't supposed to be there.

I look back at the dock. My father stands watching me. The teenage boy is renting another kayak, probably one that works. I always get broken things. Last time we went skiing, I got broken poles that made me fall down. I am determined to conquer this kayak. I plunge my paddle into the water again. The kayak only turns in circles. I am never going to get out to where the sailboats are. I am never going to get out to the blue, blue water. I swear I can hear the kayak laughing at me. "Stupid kayak!" I yell in frustration. I hit the front of the boat with the paddle. I consider using my hands to paddle, the way I do on a raft in the pool. The boat drifts back to the swimming section, and the lifeguard whistles again. The older kids tanning themselves on the raft turn to look at me. Everyone is waving me away. The paddle flails in my hand. I look helplessly back to the dock.

I hear someone laughing. My father is sitting down, holding his sides, laughing. The teenage boy is calmly drinking a Coke. My father is almost crying with laughter. "It's broken," I yell, but he cups his ear like he can't hear me. I glare angrily at the red kayak. In desperation I paddle backward. That seems to work. I edge away from the swimming area, but when I try to go forward, I head right back to the danger zone. The stupid kayak will only go backward! I end up paddling it backward all the way to the dock.

When at last I reach safety, the teenage boy helps me out of the kayak. He doesn't say a word. The boat is rented for an hour, but I've probably been out only fifteen minutes. I don't care. I tear off the life jacket and throw it to the ground. My father is trying very hard not to laugh. He says, "I'm sorry we rented you a piece of defective equipment." I throw down the paddle and walk away. My father catches up to me and scoops me into his arms. Laughing, he throws me over his shoulders. I watch the slats of wood on the dock pass by and the glint of brown lake water between them. I can't decide whether to laugh or to cry.

"I want a Slurpee," I tell my father. I am sulking.

We walk up to the concession stand. The Slurpee machine churns bright red and bright blue ices. I choose red. My father passes it down to me with a straw. "The kayak was broken," I tell him.

"Obviously," he says. Next to the stand, a trash can overflows with Coke cans and empty Slurpee cups. There are bees swarming around the garbage. I move so my father is standing between me and the bees. I close my eyes and feel the warm sun on my face, and the taste of cold cherry Slurpee fills my mouth. My father is standing between me and the bees so I am safe; the bees can't get me.

My father is in a foul mood. He has picked a fight with my mother, and now they are arguing about something. We're not sure what set him off today. He may have lost at tennis. The Braves may have lost their baseball game. Or maybe the kitchen was messy or the water heater has broken and he can't find the warranty. We kids know to avoid him when he gets in these moods. Lately, he's prone to lose his temper even more than he used to. I know that he's put his money into something called "the building," and "the building" is not working out well. I asked my mother one night what it would take to get rid of "the building," and she said "a million dollars," and we don't have a million dollars. There are problems with my father's partners at work. One of them doesn't remember to bill the patients; another one wants to leave the practice. My mother, apparently, doesn't know the value of money. She forgets to record checks in the checkbooks. She thinks we can afford lamb chops, and we can't afford lamb chops every day of the goddamn week. I know some of their friends have already gotten divorced. Mr. Stern moved out of the house and drives a black sports car now. The Stern triplets are the same age as me and Jonathan. They live with just their mother now. Their father moved into an apartment, and he has a girlfriend. We ran into Mr. Stern and his girlfriend at the movie theater; she doesn't look like a mother. She has blond hair flipped back like Farrah Fawcett, and she wears tight jeans with gold piping down the sides and pink frosted lipstick. She looks like the girls who work at the makeup counters in the mall.

When my father starts to yell, my brothers and I retreat to our hiding places. My older brother goes to a spacious closet under the basement stairs, which he has turned into a fort. He has brought down flashlights and his rock collection. I am not allowed in his fort. My room has an alcove that I crawl into and, safely hidden, read a book. I have read half of the *Little House on the Prairie* series while hiding from my parents' fights. Jonathan and I are eleven years old, and Mark is fourteen. Jonathan has gone outside and over to a friend's house. Sometimes he comes into my alcove, and sometimes Mark even lets him into the fort. I hate, hate, hate it when my father yells. Sometimes I will very quietly put a record on my record player, but I am afraid to put it up too loud because I don't want him to hear me in case he's mad at me. My record player has an orange and white cover. I only have three records: *Winnie the Pooh and the Blustery Day, Joseph and the Amazing Technicolor Dreamcoat,* and a 45 of Olivia Newton-John singing "Have You Never Been Mellow." I should not have left my shoes in the den; he doesn't like it when we leave things where they don't belong. Once he threw Mark's shoes in the trash can because he got sick of looking at them. The father in *Little House on the Prairie* doesn't get mad; sometimes he gives one of the girls a serious talk, but he doesn't yell. Laura Ingalls Wilder probably never left her shoes in the den, though. I hear my father telling my mother, "We aren't rich. I know it would be so wonderful if we were rich and could just give loans to the cleaning lady whenever we want to. I know that would be just wonderful."

They are right outside my door. My mother doesn't answer him. If I push the carpeting on my floor one way, it looks bright blue, but if I push it the other way, it looks dark blue. I left the lights off in my room so they won't know I'm in here. I wish the dog were with me, but he might make noise. My father throws things when he gets mad. You can't slide the door between the kitchen and the den closed anymore because he has slammed it so many times. He has broken his tennis racket before. Once he threw Jonathan's clarinet, but it was in its case and it didn't break. There's a hole in the wall in Mark's room where the doorknob smashed through.

This fight will end, and later we will all sit down to a silent dinner. Jonathan and I will tell a funny story about how the dog messed up the piles of leaves we were raking. Then we'll clear the table, and my father will go sit at his desk to pay bills. My brothers and I are all scared my parents are going to get a divorce, but we haven't said anything about it to each other. We are scared that if we say something about it, we will make it real.

After dinner I go down to the basement to help my mother fold the laundry. She pulls a heap of warm sheets out of the dryer and hands me a corner. The sheet smells warm and safe. I take a step back so it stretches between us. My face is flushing, but I can't stand not knowing anymore. Staring down at the sheet, I whisper, "Are you and Dad going to get a divorce?"

"I don't know," she answers. "Maybe." I step forward and hand her my half of the folded sheet. We finish folding the towels and sheets in silence.

I go back upstairs to finish my homework. We are studying Africa in social studies. I have a brand-new social studies book, and I love the way it smells. It has pictures of gazelles and giraffes and a man with makeup on his face. The leading exports of Africa, the book tells me, are diamonds, oil, and rubber. There are more than three hundred different languages in Africa. Someone knocks on my door. My father says, "Can I talk to you for a minute?" I know this is because I asked my mother about the divorce, and I really don't want to talk about it. "I'm studying," I tell him. "We have a test on Wednesday."

"It won't take long," he says.

I sigh and close my book. I follow him downstairs and out to the porch where we sit next to each other on a green couch. I stare straight ahead, but I can smell his smell of soap and sweat and freshly cut grass. He has grown a beard, and he rubs it when he talks.

"I think you've figured out that things are a little difficult right now with your mother and me," he says, "but we're trying to work things out." I can feel him looking at me, but

I don't look at him. He raises one hand to touch my hair, and I pull away. "No matter what happens," he says, "you'll always be my little girl."

I shrug my shoulders. "I have to study," I say. "We have a test on Wednesday."

My father tries to hug me, but I sit there stiffly. I am aware that he is next to me and that he would like to hold me, but I don't want him to. I don't feel safe with him there. I feel weird. I just want to go back to my room and study more about Africa. I get up and walk away.

I am fifteen years old, and my head is a volcano. Crusted blisters erupt from the right side of my forehead and spill down toward my eyes. I am so hideous that I cannot stand to look at myself in the mirror, and I have covered the mirrors in my bedroom and the bathroom with a sheet. I have shingles. It is the most bizarre thing that has ever happened to me. I don't even know what shingles are; the only shingles I know about are on the sides of houses. In a sharp line down the center of my forehead and over my eyebrow, there are thick blisters draining blood and water. They alternately itch and burn, and I feel terrible. I cannot eat. My eye is almost swollen shut. I have no idea what is happening to me, but different doctors come to see me every day, all friends of my father, and they are all worried.

Every night I sit in my room in darkness. I don't want to see anybody or anything. I keep my eyes shut tight. When my father comes home from work, I can hear him climb the stairs, and I hear him talking to my mother outside the room. She tells him what I ate, if I got out of bed, if she thinks I'm getting better or worse. He comes into my room

and sits at the edge of my bed. He is still in a coat and tie
and smells like the hospital. He fishes out some swabs. He
has to place his hand around my head and pry my swollen
eye open so that he can wipe away some of the crust. I
don't see how he can bear to touch me, I'm so repulsive. I
know that he is worried that the infection will spread into
my eye. I heard him tell my mother that if this happens, it
would be very bad. He is always reminding me not to
scratch the blisters, and if I do scratch, I have to wash my
hands right away. He is worried that, if the infection
spreads, I could end up blind in one eye, but he doesn't tell
me this.

There isn't much anyone can do but wait and watch. In
1980 there is no treatment for shingles. My father asks if I've
managed to do any schoolwork. He is trying to act normal.
He doesn't know why I have the shingles. I had a good case
of chicken pox when I was seven years old, and I ought to
be immune to the virus that causes shingles. My father is a
doctor, and he knows that most people who get shingles are
either old or very sick or both. I am neither. The shingles
have interrupted track season. My parents will finally attrib-
ute it to stress. I will go back to tenth grade and get caught
up in my classes, and except for some fine scars over my
eyelid, there won't be anything left to remind us that it
happened.

My father is furious at me because I ate a peanut. We are
driving in his car together, on our way to the hospital where
I am supposed to have surgery. We have been waiting all
day for this surgery, and out of desperate hunger, I popped
a peanut into my mouth. One peanut. I only did it when it
was so late in the day, it seemed that I wouldn't be having

surgery after all. As soon as I ate the peanut, the phone rang telling us to come to the hospital.

I need surgery because there is so much swelling in my head that my ears are blocked off. Fluid cannot drain, and I can hear only 30 percent of what a normal person hears. I had a hearing test a week ago that showed this fact. For the past year, I have been having unusual problems. I have had throat infections almost every month. The glands under my jaw are swollen; they stay swollen even when I take antibiotics. There are warts all over my legs, and no one seems to be able to make them go away. My father has sent me to different doctors, an allergist, an ear-nose-and-throat doctor, an infectious disease doctor, a dermatologist. None of them can figure out what is wrong with me. At the university infirmary, they just keep saying I have mono. If that is the case, I have had mono for a year and a half. My father is worried in general about my health, and now I've gone and eaten a peanut.

I wasn't going to mention the peanut to my father, but then I thought maybe I should. "Does it matter if I ate a peanut?" I ask casually.

"What?" his voice rises. "You did what?" He is panicking.

"I ate a peanut," I say, trying to smile. "Just one."

"Oh, my God," he says. "How well did you chew it?"

This whole thing strikes me as ridiculous. As well as one generally chews a peanut, I think. I shrug. "Pretty well," I say.

"They might not be able to do the surgery," he tells me. "This could be a total disaster."

I know now that a peanut is about the worst thing to eat right before surgery. Under general anesthesia, it can get coughed up in the stomach and then swallowed down the windpipe, stuck in the trachea, causing asphyxiation. Small children choke to death on peanuts by this very mechanism.

"We'll have to tell the anesthesiologist about this," he continues. "He may not want to put you to sleep. If I were him, I probably wouldn't do it."

I am finding this whole thing kind of funny. How can life-and-death matters hinge on a peanut? "If I die," I tell him, "you have to sing 'Found a Peanut' at the funeral."

"This is not funny," my father says. "Not funny at all."

At the hospital, my father walks with me into the pre-op area. He tells the nurse we need to talk to the anesthesiologist before we do anything. A doctor comes out in green scrubs with a green paper cap on his head and a mask untied around his neck. He says, "Hello, Evan," and shakes my father's hand.

My father says, gravely, "She ate a peanut."

"Oh," the doctor says. They both look at me without amusement. The doctor says, "We'll have to take some special precautions."

The surgery turns out fine. I do not choke on the peanut. My throat is sore from the tube the doctor put down it, apparently an extra-large one so they could go after the peanut if it decided to come back up. My ears ache deep inside a little, and they feel big from the numbing medicine. Other than that, I feel well, except that the world is suddenly crashing and roaring with noise. My father drives me home, and I marvel at my newly restored hearing. All the normal background noises of life are practically deafening, the birds in the trees and the slamming of car doors, the Doppler whoosh of trucks passing on the highway, the static on the radio. I have heard none of this for three months, and the air suddenly crackles with these sounds. I share this revelation with my father, but he only frowns. "You mean you haven't heard any of this?" he asks.

I shake my head no. He doesn't see the wonder in what I am experiencing because he is deeply distressed that I lost my hearing in the first place. This is not an exciting new experience; this is frightening. He recognizes that restoring my hearing with tubes in my ears is only treating a symptom. We still do not know why my glands are so swollen. No one has mono for eighteen months. He is starting to think his daughter has more than a cold, more even than a bizarre case of shingles. He is starting to think there is something gravely wrong with my body.

Recently I was sorting through a stack of my old medical records. All the papers, notes and letters from doctors, various blood tests and X-rays, read like an odd sort of travel log, a record of my peripatetic wanderings from hospital to hospital in search of a diagnosis and a treatment for my illness. I had never seen many of these documents, and I was most struck by two letters, one from Dr. Jacobson at Massachusetts General Hospital, where my first comprehensive evaluation was done during my last year of college, and another from Dr. Ralph Shapiro at the University of Minnesota, to whom I was referred by Dr. Jacobson. In the first, Dr. Jacobson explains to Dr. Shapiro that he is convinced I will soon develop lymphoma—cancer of the lymph nodes—indeed, he is not entirely convinced that I don't already have it. In the second, Dr. Shapiro responds to Dr. Jacobson that he expects I will either develop lymphoma, as Dr. Jacobson predicted, or cancer of the nose and throat. By the time I read these letters, I knew that these risks existed. I also had the benefit of knowing that I had lived thirteen long years since the first predictions. In other words, rumors of my imminent demise appeared to be greatly exaggerated. What struck me, however, was that in both letters, the doctors clearly state that they have shared these prognoses with my father.

I am in a pleasant room in Aspen Valley Hospital, in more pain than I have ever known in the twenty-six years of my life. The room has a large window with a view of mountains, blue-white with fresh snow. I cannot appreciate the view. My throat feels as if it has been ripped from my body, shredded with a metal grater, trampled and then sewn back in with a rusty needle. My mouth is full of fluid—my own spit—that I can't swallow, so I let it drool out into a cup. My arms are bruised from a series of IVs and needle sticks. I have not eaten in days. Fluids and antibiotics are pouring into my veins to sustain me.

We are supposed to be on a family ski vacation, but after one day of skiing, I developed fevers and chills. After two days, I couldn't swallow. My father decided I needed to be admitted to the hospital. He and the doctor at Aspen Valley Hospital agreed that, especially given the Colorado altitude, I was at risk for dehydration. For four days the doctors have remained puzzled. My father has explained that I have a problem with my immune system. He is worried that I have a fungal infection in my throat. The doctors have run tests looking for such an infection, but so far they haven't found anything. He and the doctors discuss which antibiotics to give me. They stand at my bedside and talk in a language I don't understand about things like "cultures" and "obstruction," words for which I know meanings, but not in the context they are using them.

I have not improved with any of the antibiotics they have thrown at me. Instead, I have gotten worse; I have needed greater and greater doses of pain medication, and I am sinking deeper and deeper into sickness. My father is confused and frustrated. During the day, he skis with Mark, whose vacation my parents don't want to ruin; he gets only two weeks a year. My father thinks of possible tests to run while they ride the ski lift. He stops at the lodge on the way down the mountain, holds a pay phone in his mittened hands, and calls the hospital to ask how I am doing. He has my mother put the nurse on the phone so he can get my lab results.

My parents take turns sitting by my bedside. They beg me to get out of bed and walk; they try to coax me to swallow food, but I cannot do it. I take a small bite of Jell-O, hold it in my mouth, count to three, and try to swallow, but it is like counting to three and then trying to hit your thumb with a hammer. I cannot force myself to do it. I lie in bed and beg to be allowed to die. I don't know what is happening to me; I only know it hurts.

Finally, after four days, the doctors figure out that I have a herpes simplex infection stretching from the back of my mouth all the way down my esophagus. My entire throat is blistered and raw. This would explain my terrible pain. They start me on acyclovir, the appropriate medication, just one day before the vacation is over, but it will take a while before I feel better. Meanwhile the week is up. The vacation has been ruined, and my family has to get me home. I don't want to move. I don't want to go anywhere at all.

My parents have decided that I have to go home with them, even though I am now living in New York. I will need several more days of hospitalization and then home treatment. They do not expect me to be better for at least two weeks. My mother has sat by my bedside for days, and she is exhausted. She needs to go home where she has friends who can help her. My father wants me in a bigger hospital. Aspen Valley Hospital is a great place to go if you break a leg, but it is not the best hospital for obscure illnesses.

My mother tells me that the next day I will have to get out of bed and into a car for the two-hour drive to Denver. I will then have to get on a plane and fly to Atlanta. I don't have a choice. I am just going to have to do it.

I tell her no.

My mother tells me she can't let me stay in the hospital alone. She cannot bear the thought of it.

I tell her I am an adult, and I can make my own decisions. I am in too much pain to move. I can't go anywhere.

"Please," my mother begs me. I shake my head.

She goes to get my father. I hear her tell him, "She says she won't go."

My father tells me, "You're leaving with us tomorrow whether you like it or not." He is trying to be serious, but he looks clownish in his red powder pants and bulky après ski boots. His face is burned red with white circles around his eyes from the ski goggles. He stands with his arms crossed by my bedside. He knows what it means to be diagnosed with a herpes infection in the throat. It means you have basically got only the remnants of an immune system. Healthy twenty-six-year-olds do not get infections like this. Such infections are seen only in HIV patients, in cancer patients whose immune systems have been destroyed by chemotherapy, and in the very old and decrepit. The fact that I have this infection tells my father that my body is shattered. It tells my father that I am going to die, probably soon. Soon an infection will take hold and overwhelm me, if not this one then the next, or the one after that. He is now convinced that his daughter has a death sentence.

My father tells me, "There's not going to be any discussion on this. Your mother's tired. She needs to go home, and you have to go with us."

"I can't do it," I say. I turn my face to the giant window. The sun is setting, and the mountains glow orange. "I have to stay here."

I don't want to look at my father, but I can feel him staring at me. "We'll settle this tomorrow," he announces.

The next morning my father comes into my room. I close my eyes and pretend to be asleep. Maybe he won't want to wake me up. He turns the lights on and says, "Get up." I still do not open my eyes. He stands over my bed. "Get up," he says calmly. I reluctantly open my eyes. My father is carrying a pair of pants, a shirt, and a sweater. He throws them onto the bed and tells me to put them on. He says, "Get dressed, or I will pick you up and carry you to the car in that hospital gown. You have to go home. You have to get to a better hospital."

"I'm not going," I insist.

My father leaves the room. He comes back in with a nurse. "Give her a shot of morphine," he says. "And take out the IV." The nurse looks confused.

"I don't want to go," I cry. "I want to sleep. I'm tired."

My father pulls back the bed sheets. He looks at me dispassionately. "This is something that has to be done," he says. I don't move.

"Don't make me carry you," he says.

I start to cry. "You are very sick," he says, "and you have to come home." His voice is absolutely flat, clinical. He looks at me from a great distance away, as if he were appraising something he just found in the road. "You cannot stay here."

I am stunned. I am in too much pain to move; my father

should be able to appreciate this simple fact. I can't move. I can't. I hear my father's voice again; it sounds as if it were coming from far away. "Jamie," he says, "get dressed."

Slowly I sit up in bed and reach for my shirt. The nurse gives me a last dose of painkiller. I feel it run up my arm, fuzzy and warm like an animal. Then I put on my shirt, a sweater, a jacket. The nurse brings a wheelchair, and they take me out to the car.

My father doesn't say a word to me as I struggle into the front seat. I am wearing normal clothes, but I haven't brushed my teeth or combed my hair in days. I catch a glimpse of myself in the rearview mirror; I look like a drug addict. My face is washed out and pale, with dark thumb-sized bruises under my eyes. My brother and my mother sit in the backseat; my father tilts my seat so I can lie down. All the way to the airport, he keeps switching his eyes from the road to me. The mountain roads are twisty, and I can feel the car swerve and loop. In the backseat, my brother clears his throat and says, "Uh—why don't you keep your eyes on the road?" My throat hurts so badly, I want to die. My father feels that if he can just keep looking at me, I won't die between here and the airplane, between the airplane and the hospital at home. If he can keep looking at me forever, if he never shuts his eyes, I won't die.

I am filling out medical school applications while I recuperate from my first parotid surgery. There is a chain of stitches up the back of my neck, and I feel a tug every time I smile, but other than that I'm feeling pretty good for someone who just had major surgery. I've moved into my own apartment in Atlanta. I'm going to do a year of molecular biology research before going to medical school. For the past two years, I've been receiving intravenous gamma globulin treatments and giving myself shots of interferon. I've had one parotid infection during that time, but overall I've felt well. I've learned chemistry and biology; I've read up on my illness. Dr. Cunningham-Rundles, the immunologist in New York who has been responsible for my remarkable recovery, thinks I have a natural-killer-cell defect, and I've read textbooks and articles to learn what natural killer cells are. Someday I hope to do my own research on them.

My dog likes the new apartment; it has a big shady backyard, and there is a black Labrador retriever in the yard next door to converse with. The apartment is gigantic by New York standards, two bedrooms and two bathrooms. I actually have room for an office. My computer is set up. I've given myself a year to write a novel, but before I write the novel, I have to write 250 words on why I want to be a doctor.

The phone rings. It's my father. He and my mother want to come over and have dinner with me. They have something to discuss with me. I shrug. I don't know many people in Atlanta yet, and for the moment my parents are my main social life.

When my parents arrive, they aren't smiling. My father tells me he needs to talk to me about something serious. He and my mother sit on the couch. I sit on the floor with my dog. My father says, "Dr. Gussack called with the pathology results from your surgery." My dog rolls onto his back to make his stomach more accessible to scratching. "The pathology shows that you have cancer."

I scratch the dog. "Did they do flow cytometry?" I ask.

"I don't think so," my father says. His eyes are fixed on the floor. My mother's eyes are fixed on the dog.

"They can't know for sure until they do the flow," I tell

him. "They were confused by the basic pathology at Mass General, too. You can't tell what's going on just by looking at the microscope. I don't think they can say for sure I have cancer yet."

"That's not what Dr. Gussack said," my father insists.

"I know," I say, "but he's not a hematologist. Don't panic yet." I know I cannot truly reassure him. I realize that he's heard this diagnosis so many times, he's probably thinking that at some point it will have to be true. He trusts Dr. Gussack; they are colleagues, and after waiting so long for dreaded news, it is easier to accept it than deny it. But I've reviewed my records; I've read my pathology reports; I've discussed my medical history at length with Dr. Cunningham-Rundles, and I know that special tests have to be done before a diagnosis of lymphoma can be made definitively. It strikes me suddenly that I know more about my illness than my father does.

I look at him with love and pity. He isn't young anymore. In pictures from Salt Lake City when I was born, he was just a kid, with a goofy smile, a crew cut, and a Volkswagen Beetle. Now he has streaks of gray in his hair; there are deep laugh lines around his eyes that are visible even when he isn't laughing. When he walks, his shoulders are stooped, and his knees are stiff. Blue ropy veins twist on the back of his hand.

"Don't worry," I repeat, but my father has been worrying for a lifetime about various things and, for the last ten years, mainly about me. I can see that he is not reassured. I can see that his mind has already ticked ahead to where I am having chemotherapy, to where I am living at home, with a bald head, vomiting from toxic medicines. He has already envisioned me in a hospital bed, receiving medications through my arm, skeletal and washed out, exhausted and ready to die. He is already picturing nights in the intensive care unit, completing a living will and having to make a decision about whether to continue life support; he is thinking of what it will be like to make the decision to stop the ventilator, to attend his daughter's funeral, to hear her eulogy. He has watched the children of other friends die, one from cancer, one from muscular dystrophy, and he sees no reason why he should be spared this agony. He has stood and watched it, and now he fears he is going to have to endure it himself.

I turn out to be right. Further tests show that I do not have cancer. Instead of starting chemotherapy, I start medical school. I come to know far more about immune deficiencies than my father does. I find my own doctors at Emory University and begin making my own decisions about my health care. All through medical school and most of internship, I stay healthy. I study hard and fall in love and get married. I learn to navigate the insurance industry; my monthly infusions are as normal to my life as going to church on Sunday is for other people. My nurses and doctors are my colleagues and friends. I have relieved my father of the double burden of not only loving me while I am sick but also having to be my doctor.

My father is a changed man. He takes pleasure in his daily life, and he considers himself happier now than he ever has been in his life. On the surface, little has changed. My parents live in the same house in which I grew up. My father still drives a Toyota and has a modest practice. Some colleagues have retired; some have made millions. But he is content. He is willing to spend the money he has carefully saved, not extravagantly, but on little luxuries, bicycle trips and beach vacations for the whole family. He has embraced a political cause: after watching me struggle with health insurance, he wants a national health care plan, and he valiantly defends this idea to his private practice colleagues, most of whom are horrified by anything that smacks of socialism. He flies to Washington, D.C., and meets with politicians. He attends meetings for Physicians for a National Health Care Plan and lectures at grand rounds. He still loves baseball; he shares season tickets and sits high in the stands behind home plate, admiring the emerald green diamond. Every Saturday morning and Wednesday afternoon, he plays tennis. After years of being the class clown, he decides to take a course on stand-up comedy. He enjoys it so much, he does it twice.

He is content. His twins are both married; last fall Jonathan gave him a granddaughter. This summer my father spent an afternoon painting a room of my house with Victor. My father brought over a portable television set so he could watch the baseball game while they worked. My mother and I went shopping. When we came back, we all went out for hamburgers at the local pub, and my father had a beer. He said it was a perfect day.

My father wakes up early one morning in April with a sense of dread. Normally on a Saturday morning in the spring, he would have a breakfast of instant coffee and Quaker Oat Squares with blueberries and skim milk. Then he would take his tennis racket and a can of fresh yellow tennis balls and head to the neighborhood tennis club, six courts exposed to the unforgiving Atlanta sun, next to a scrubby baseball field and a swimming pool that won't be open for the season until Memorial Day. At the courts, he would meet up with his tennis buddies.

He has been playing tennis with some of these men for

almost forty years. Over that time, they've married; some
have divorced. Their children have grown up; some of the
children have done well, become prosperous accountants
and lawyers with families of their own. Among the children,
there has been one suicide, one death from a brain tumor,
two serious mental illnesses, and an assortment of minor triumphs and small disappointments. The tennis guys themselves are getting older. One splits his time between Atlanta
and North Carolina. Another died last year, after receiving a
lung transplant. Some are retired; some work only part time
now. They travel to distant cities to see their children and
their grandchildren. When they are home, though, they play
tennis, and they play to win.

On this Saturday morning, however, my father is not going to play tennis. After breakfast he is going to drive down
to Emory University Hospital, where I am a patient. Two
days before, I checked into the hospital with what seemed
like a minor infection. Now the infection is threatening to invade my brain. I hover in a morphine delirium, my face
swelled up to twice its normal size. Once again no one
knows what is causing the infection, and no one is sure how
to treat it.

This illness has taken my father by surprise. I have managed to stay out of the hospital for five years. For the past
five years, I have looked, for all the world, like a normal
person, and slowly, gradually, my father has let go of some
of the worry that grew and thrived on letters from doctors
with cancer predictions and long nights in Colorado and
Massachusetts hospitals and surgeries and swollen glands.

I am half asleep when my father comes into the room. My
eyes are closed, but I know it is him by the shuffle of his
feet. He closes the door gently behind him; he doesn't want
to wake me. The TV is on but muted. The blinds are open.

The sky is brittle and blue. An IV pump clicks. Last night, finally, the doctors started me on the correct medications, and my fever has broken. I am actually getting better. The worst is over.

My father doesn't see this. He looks down at his daughter's face, swollen and bruised. He recognizes her there, through the blows and wounds that disease has wrought, and he sees at once a bald-headed, big-eyed baby, a one-year-old in a pink snowsuit learning to walk, a five-year-old riding a purple bike with training wheels, a ten-year-old dressed like a princess, a fifteen-year-old in her mother's suit at a debate contest. He sees me at twenty-one, short hair dyed red, graduating from college; at thirty-one in a white wedding dress, a hand on his shoulder as we dance a rigid waltz. And now he sees me at thirty-three, eyes shut, mouth forced open, arms black and bruised from needle sticks.

Through my half-sleep, I hear a sound croak from my father, a sob. He collapses into a chair and drops his head in his hands. He tries to muffle his cries. I have never, in my entire life, seen my father cry.

I sit up. I say, "Dad, Dad. It's okay. I'll be okay."

He is embarrassed that I have seen him. He doesn't want me to know how scared he is. He doesn't want to scare me. I get out of bed, trailing my IV pole, and put a hand on his shoulder. "I'm getting better," I tell him. "I'm going to be fine."

"I know," he says, "I know you will. It's just—I can't lose you."

BEGETTING

The night before the presidential election of 2000, I did not sleep well. I tossed and turned, made frequent trips to the bathroom, drank several glasses of water, and finally gave up on sleep and got out of bed before sunrise. All night I felt as if I had a bowling ball in my belly, rocking heavily back and forth and pressing down on my bladder. It was not surprising that I felt this way. I was thirty-nine weeks pregnant. I had reached the point where I felt comfortable only in the bathtub, even though our tub was not deep enough to cover my stomach entirely, and the top of it stuck out like an island. My belly button had popped out, a sign my friend Sally said meant that the baby was cooked, like the thermometer popping out of the turkey in the oven. "Any day now," she warned me.

On the morning of election day, I sat in my bathrobe and slippers on the front porch. The sky was turning an inky blue, with light seeping up from the asphalt and from behind the neat little houses on our street. I watched Roy, my old black Bernese mountain dog, limp down the stairs and sniff along the sidewalk. The baby kicked. I placed my hands on my abdomen; the skin was stretched tight, but it was thick and leathery, not soft like the skin on my arms. When I pressed down, I could feel the firm curves of my baby's body, but I could only guess what they corresponded to. The doctor said her head was down in my pelvis, so I guessed at whether what I felt under my hands was the curve of her butt, the angle of a knee, the hard edge of a foot. When I let go, she floated back into place.

For weeks I had been wanting to reach inside myself and take the baby out. Only for a moment, I told my husband, just to make sure she was all right. Just to count her fingers and toes. Just to make sure her head was the right size, that the organs were tucked away in the right order in her chest and belly, that her eyes could open and her ears were the right shape and her heart pumped with four chambers, as it should, and her legs were the same length and her brain worked and she could breathe. If I could just make sure she was all right, I would be happy to let her float in the warm safety of my body for another two weeks, even another month.

I had a doctor's appointment that morning, just a checkup. As far as I could tell, I showed no signs of labor. The doctors had been asking me if I could feel my uterus tightening. They asked if it felt like the baby had dropped. They asked if I had been breathing more easily. I didn't know how to answer them. I knew they were trying to assess where I was in the process of incubating a baby. I had asked pregnant women these questions myself, as a medical student and an intern, but I had not realized how difficult they were to answer. Was my uterus tightening? I didn't know. I felt a hundred different things, but I could not put a name to any of them. I could not distinguish the baby's wriggling from a false contraction. I had no idea where in my body the baby lay. I had never felt any of these things before, so when the doctor asked if I felt a contraction, she might as well have asked me if I felt the wings of angels on my face. It was all equally abstract and dreamy.

My husband was still asleep when I left the house. I whispered to him that we would vote when I got back from the doctor's office. My suitcase was packed and had been sitting by the door for the past two weeks. Unlike with my many previous hospitalizations, I had enjoyed packing for this one. The suitcase contained all the things the books had recommended we bring to the hospital: two pairs of pajamas, a blue flannel bathrobe, a pair of my husband's socks, five compact discs, massage oil, toothbrush and toothpaste, one newborn onesie, one tiny hat, one yellow baby blanket, sanitary napkins, and newborn diapers. It did not occur to me to take the suitcase. I drove to the doctor's office, climbed the stairs in the parking lot, and waited in her waiting room, reading the October issue of *Parents* magazine, which had detailed descriptions of how to make your own Halloween costumes. A fat baby boy was dressed as a bumble bee in yellow and black stripes with antennae made of pipe cleaners and Styrofoam springing from his head. There were other pregnant women in the room, and we smiled at one another as if we were all in on a great secret. One woman took large gulps from a bottle of water. Another slipped off her shoes and rubbed her feet.

The nurse called me back, weighed me, directed me to the bathroom for the usual urine sample, and then advised me to wait in room eight. She bustled into room eight soon after me, proffered the paper gown and bustled out, returned again, squirted cold blue jelly onto my stomach, and waved around the microphone end of the Doppler machine to pick up the baby's heartbeat. *Shoo-shoo-shoo-shoo-shoo* it thumped rapidly, so different from an adult heartbeat where the *lub* and the *dub* take their time, dripping steadily, the second sound a little deeper and stronger than the first. "Sounds healthy." The nurse smiled as she wiped off the blue jelly. She told me to relax. "Dr. Fisch will be here in a minute."

I lay on my back studying the tiles on the ceiling. Dr. Fisch, Jacqui, was my good friend. I had chosen her because I had expected this pregnancy to be complex, given all my health issues, and I wanted someone who would be willing to make the extra phone call, to think a little harder, to take her time with me. To our great surprise, the pregnancy had been, in her word, "uneventful," and we had reached thirty-nine weeks safely, so that now I waited, like any other pregnant woman, for labor to begin.

Jacqui came into the room. "How *are* you feeling?" she asked earnestly.

I shrugged. I was wearing a white crepe paper gown, and she was dressed, as always, impeccably, in a black pantsuit. Even when she was a resident and had been up all night delivering babies at the city hospital, Jacqui always looked perfectly rested, with every hair in place, lipstick unsmudged, smelling like a rose in her green surgical scrubs.

"I don't feel very different," I said. "I just feel like there's a bowling ball in my bladder."

"A bowling ball," Jacqui repeated, drawling out the *o* in *bowling* with her elegant South African accent. "Well, let's see what the cervix is doing. It sounds like we may end up inducing you."

I lay back on the table, and Jacqui put her gloved hand inside me. She pushed the bowling ball back up against my ribs, and I had to take short breaths. She eased her hand back out of me and snapped off her gloves. "Jamie," she said calmly, "you are 5 centimeters dilated and 50 percent effaced. Darling, you are in labor."

I have always known that I wanted to have children. As a baby-sitter, I was a veritable Mary Poppins. To get the kids to clean up their rooms, I would have them pretend that we were all windup toys. I would twist an imaginary key in their backs, and then, all wound up, we'd run around putting away toys and making beds. After a few minutes, they'd wind down and droop over, and I would have to run over and wind them back up again. I made up treasure hunts with maps and secret codes. I added food coloring to spaghetti to turn it purple and green. As I got older, my friends had children, and I continued to play these games. I climbed trees; I pushed swings; I acted out stories. I curtsied to fairy princesses and cowered in awe before Power Rangers and played peekaboo with infants in the grocery store. On my pediatrics rotation, I volunteered to change diapers, give the babies their bottles, take a turn in the playroom.

Despite my full awareness of my medical condition, it

never occurred to me that I might not be able to have children. Naïvely, I assumed I would stop using birth control, and in a matter of months, I'd conceive a child. I knew there were some issues to explore. Before Victor and I started trying to conceive, I flew to New York to see Dr. Cunningham-Rundles. As usual she saw me with a host of the fellows and residents that she was teaching in the room. As she and I spoke, they stood awkwardly behind her and tried to pretend they were not there. I smiled at them, because I have stood awkwardly in the corner behind attending physicians so many times myself. I brought up the issue of pregnancy, and she thought for a moment. Charlotte is a mother herself, and I felt certain she understood how much I wanted a child. She told me she saw no overwhelming risk to my health. "But," she answered honestly, "I can't tell you for sure. No one has any experience with this. What you have is so rare. We still haven't found the defect in your immune system." She turned to the residents and fellows behind her. "What do you tell a patient in this situation?" she asked them. No one answered, so she answered for them. "All you can do is be honest. You've reached the limits of medical knowledge."

It is not known what effects interferon might have on a developing fetus. Dr. Cunningham-Rundles felt it would be best if I stopped the medication for two months before conceiving and at least for the first trimester of the pregnancy. I knew that without interferon, I'd be vulnerable to viruses again, and so I'd get warts all up and down my legs and my lymph nodes would be even more swollen than usual. I also knew that these problems would go away again, once I resumed the injections. But no one could say what other problems might arise, either in the short term or the long term, from my not taking interferon for several months. It might increase my risk of developing cancer or a serious infection, but taking it might cause long-term harm to the baby. I had to choose between doing what we felt was safest for the baby and what was safest for myself. I chose the health of the baby.

Because of the risk of cervical cancer, I also discussed pregnancy with Dr. Horowitz, my gynecological oncologist, who had performed a number of procedures on my cervix to prevent the development of cancer. He was concerned about stopping interferon, since it controlled not only the warts on my legs, which were ugly but not a serious threat to my health, but also the warts on my cervix, which were invisible but potentially deadly, since they can cause cancer. But he assured me that none of the procedures he had performed on me in the past would endanger the pregnancy and that, even if I were to develop cervical cancer, it would progress slowly. It was an odd sort of reassurance, but he said, "Worst-case scenario: you get invasive cervical cancer while you're pregnant, and after you deliver, we do a hysterectomy. You're not going to die," he promised.

I asked him what would happen if the cancer developed on the vaginal side wall instead of the uterus.

"Okay," he said in his Brooklyn accent, muted now by years spent in the South, "then we do a vulvectomy."

"A vulvectomy." When I was a medical student, I had watched Dr. Horowitz perform this surgery. Basically the woman's pelvis is hollowed out. Her uterus, cervix, and vagina are all removed, and then she is reconstructed, cobbled together like an unsteady tent, with tissue pulled down from her hips and abdomen. It takes hours to tie off all the arteries and cut out all the organs until only an empty cave is left.

He saw my face blanch. "We're not doing a vulvectomy," he said. "You're going to be fine. Go make a baby."

I stopped giving myself interferon shots. Over the course of weeks, the warts on my legs blossomed. Where before there had only been faint tan spots, like freckles, now warts rose up, not only on my legs but on my arms, in my armpits, even a few on my face. I stopped wearing shorts. I bought tights to wear to the gym. I asked my husband if he found me repulsive. He answered honestly, "It's not the most beautiful thing I've ever seen. But it isn't going to last forever. You'll get pregnant, and in nine months you can go back on interferon." It ended up taking a lot longer than that.

At first it was fun trying to get pregnant. We made sure to have sex somewhere around the middle of my cycle, and I waited to see if I got my period. I kept getting my period, so we started to take the process more seriously. I bought ovulation predictor kits to tell me when I was most fertile, and we had sex on those days. Even if one or both of us were tired, we had sex. I still got my period, month after month, until we had failed to conceive a child after one year of trying, which meant, by definition, that either Victor or I was infertile. I asked Dr. Cunningham-Rundles if my immune deficiency caused the infertility. She did not know. She pointed out that infertility is a much more common problem than immune deficiency. It was more likely, I concluded, that I was just doubly cursed, with a faulty immune system and a faulty reproductive system.

We started the workup for infertility. My hormone levels were normal. I had dye shot into my uterus to make sure the anatomy was normal and the fallopian tubes were open. A piece of my uterus was torn out and examined under the microscope. Victor's sperm were counted and examined; they were numerous, and under the microscope the little guys swam like Olympians. The infertility doctor did not know why I was not getting pregnant. She gave me pills to take. She examined my ovaries with ultrasound and saw that I was making follicles. In the middle of my cycle, when I ovulated, the doctor took Victor's sperm and put it directly into my uterus. I did not get pregnant. She did it again in January. I did not get pregnant. She did it again in February. I did not get pregnant.

Then it was March, and I was working in the pediatric emergency room, and I got my last parotid infection. The heavy doses of narcotics and some of the antibiotics I required could have seriously damaged a fetus, as could the two CT scans and radiation I was exposed to. I thanked God that I was not pregnant so that I did not have to choose between protecting my baby and saving my life.

After I left the hospital, I went to my parents' house to recuperate. I sat on the deck amid the flowers. Victor was on a photography assignment in Peru, and my parents were out of the house. I was by myself. It was early spring, and I watched the birds flock to the intricate bird feeder that my father attended with care, the latest in a series of feeders designed to outsmart the wily squirrels who gathered on the branches around it, plotting ways to reach its treasure of seed and corn. The trees in the backyard were dusted with tender, pale green leaves. It was cool, but warm with the sun on your face, and it was the kind of day that makes you happy to be alive.

I looked at my arms, where mustard-yellow and brown bruises from all the intravenous needles were still healing. I touched the hot mesh of my swollen cheek. I started to cry. How could I have a child when my hold on life was so slim? What if I had a serious illness while I was pregnant and lost the child or caused irreparable damage to it? What if I passed this disease on to my child? I should explain to my husband that we should not have children. I should let him divorce me so that he could have a family.

My mother opened the sliding glass door and saw my tears. She did not have to ask why I was crying. She said, "I've been expecting this."

"I want to have children," I told her.

"You could adopt," she said. She corrected herself. "You *should* adopt."

I stared at her. She was holding a glass of ice water. Her face was flushed; she'd just returned from jogging. For years she'd been half-joking, half-whining about wanting to be a grandmother. At my age, she had had three children, the oldest thirteen and the youngest ten. I could tell from the certainty with which she said I should adopt that she and my father had been talking it over. I knew that this last illness had shaken them, but I saw at that moment how deeply scared they had been. They did not want anything to threaten the delicate equilibrium in my body. If they could, they would have put me behind glass.

"I don't want to adopt," I said.

"No one *wants* to adopt. People have to. And they wind up with beautiful families."

"But I want to be pregnant. I want to experience pregnancy."

"It's overrated," my mother said. "You want to have morning sickness?"

"Yes," I said. "And heartburn and back pain. I want to waddle. I want to feel the baby kick inside me. I want my breasts to hurt. I want to heave myself up out of a chair. I want to sit in a bathtub like a beached whale."

"You can't have everything. You can't risk your health for that."

"Anyway, what if I have a child and then I die?"

"That's why you have to adopt," she said. "So you don't die." She studied me. "Believe me," she said, "the most important thing to us, to me and Dad, is that you remain alive. It doesn't matter if you have a child."

"But I want to be a mother."

"I understand," she said. "I know you do. And you will. Any mother can die. If we thought about that too much, we'd all be too scared to leave the house."

A goldfinch landed on the top of the bird feeder and waited for a blue jay to finish eating. The blue jay took his time. "But," I said, "I'm more likely to . . . It doesn't seem right. It doesn't seem fair to take that chance."

My mother could answer only with platitudes. Life is full of chances. Life is not fair. More goldfinches gathered around the bird feeder. I might not have children. I might never be pregnant. The injustice of it sopped over me, and I tried not to cry. How much of life was I supposed to give up and still keep loving it?

"You need to concentrate on getting better," she said. She stood up and went into the kitchen, then returned with a bowl of ice cream.

When I was a child, I was terrified my parents would die. This fear was entirely baseless. My parents were young and healthy. I don't remember them having so much as a cold. My father played tennis twice a week. My mother jogged. One year they left us with a baby-sitter and went on vacation in Bermuda for a week. They were supposed to call when they reached Bermuda, but a hurricane the week before had knocked down the phone lines at their hotel. I spent the entire week convinced they had disappeared into the Bermuda Triangle. If I had such fears with healthy parents, what kind of fears would my child have? At some point in her life, I would probably be sick again. My child might have to visit me in the hospital; she might see me with IV lines in my arms. She would certainly know that once a month I have to go to the hospital to receive medication. She would become familiar with the small needles I use to give myself shots every other night. Her fears of losing her mother would not be nearly so baseless as mine had been. It is a mother's job to make the child feel safe and secure; how could I do that when my own life is so fragile? I touched my still swollen face. What kind of nightmares would my child have if she ever saw me as sick as I had just been, moaning in pain, my face distended to twice its normal size? The blue jay hissed at the goldfinches, and I got tired of the blue jay and threw an acorn at him to scare him away. The ice cream melted in the bowl.

I wanted my child to take me for granted. When I was a child and I was sick, my mother would set up the sea-foam green vaporizer in the room. A cloud of steam hummed out of its periscope top, and my mother sat on the side of my bed and stroked my hair. She sang "Where are you going, my little one, little one?" and brought me electric-green lime Jell-O in a bowl. She crushed my medicine into applesauce, but I could still taste it, a mix of bitter and sweet that I swallowed with feigned reluctance but really a silent kind of joy because it was the taste of love. She had a white velour robe that I used to stroke with the back of my hand until I fell asleep. She would draw a bath for me and, when I stepped out, wrap me in towels and rub me head to toe to get me warm. Later, when I began to get more seriously sick, my mother stayed home with me. She drew baths and sprinkled in baking soda to try to cool the itching when the shingles started to heal. She kept a supply of warm compresses in a metal mixing bowl by my bed, and though I couldn't open my eyes, I could hear the water trickle as she wrung them out, and I knew that moments later I would feel the cloth pressed to my forehead. She sat by my bed in Aspen and held my hand while I begged to be allowed to die. Even now, as an adult, I call for my mother when I am sick, quite unconsciously. I wanted my child to be able to call for me the same way and know that I would come, but I knew more than other people that I couldn't guarantee that for her, so maybe I shouldn't have her at all.

Off in the trees, there were nests full of baby birds. In a few months, they would be expected to fly on their own. Human beings are helpless for so much longer, and the chronically ill revisit this state of helplessness periodically, as frightened and vulnerable as baby birds. In the wake of my illness, I felt like a child again, a baby bird, and so I couldn't imagine how I could be a mother.

The cure for the fear of dying is living. My mother told me to put on shoes. We were going down to the river for a walk. At the river, Canada geese were honking overhead; they settled in a great wave on the gray rocks in the middle of the water. They took turns paddling in the water and then lifted off again, all at the same time. They were on their way north. The trail where we were walking was crowded with people, men and women in bright jogging shorts; a child passed by, tugged along by a black Lab puppy. People threw Frisbees. My mother suggested that my best friend, Claire, come down from Philadelphia for a visit. She thought it would make me feel better. That night my parents called Claire and bought her a plane ticket.

The next day Claire arrived. She and I have been best friends since freshman year of college, when we were known to push each other to class in a grocery cart. We once spent an entire afternoon trying to catch falling leaves. We look so much alike that people used to have whole conversations with me, thinking I was Claire, and vice versa. We got so used to these mix-ups that we stopped correcting the other person and just answered as if we were each other. Claire had dropped everything to come see me, abandoning Hegel and Kant. (She was in the middle of completing her philosophy Ph.D. *and* medical school.) When she arrived, she got down to the business of cheering me up. She put on a CD of Irish music and pulled me to my feet. She made me dance a jig until I laughed. It hurt my face to laugh, but I laughed. We went out for ice-cream sundaes. We got massages. We rented *Dumb and Dumber* and watched it three times, until we could recite the best lines:

"My bird died!"

"What happened?"

"His head fell off."

We ate pizza. We went shopping. We looked at pictures of ourselves in college and laughed at inside jokes that would never be funny to anyone but ourselves. The bruises on my arms healed. My face shrank back to close-to-normal size. We sat on the deck and watched the goldfinches eat. We took pity on the squirrels and tossed them handfuls of birdseed.

Claire left. Victor returned from Peru. I had surgery to remove my infected parotid gland. I finished my internship year, and Victor and I decided to try to have children again. At night we would lie in bed and discuss our options. We knew several couples who had gotten pregnant through in vitro fertilization. The procedure was becoming so common that a friend of mine actually said it seemed like the norm on the playgrounds of New York City to have twins, if not triplets. We considered a surrogate mother or adoption. Everyone had an opinion. We were told it was all stress. If we could just relax, we'd get pregnant right away. Countless people, friends and relatives, told us the story of the woman who adopted after years of infertility and then found herself pregnant. I suppose they were trying to be helpful, but it sounded as if they were somehow blaming me. I pointed out that I had treated many stressed-out crackheads who routinely got pregnant without difficulty.

My parents continued to urge me to adopt. When we went out, they would point to families with adopted children—suddenly they seemed to be everywhere—white men carrying Asian children on their shoulders, families with kids from provinces of the former Soviet Union and Romania. My mother left messages on our answering machine. "Joyce Rosenberg just adopted the most adorable little Chinese girl." She tried to appeal to my higher instincts. "You know, there are many, many unwanted baby girls in China." In the mall, my mother and I ran into an acquaintance with a little boy she'd adopted from Russia. The child looked nothing like her. She had olive skin, dark hair, and dark eyes. The boy had a round, pale face, icy blue eyes, platinum hair, ruddy cheeks, and a pug nose.

"Look how happy they are," my mother said.

I watched them walk away, the child's hand in hers. I said, "I think she has Boris Yeltsin's love child."

Victor did not want me to endanger my health, but he saw adoption as a last resort. He said he wanted a child that was made from our love, half him, half me. Ideally the child would have his calm temperament, my determination, his idealism, my pragmatism, my eyesight (he is blind without his glasses), feet (he is flat-footed), and hair (he hasn't got much left), and his height (I'm five-one on a good day), hearing, and immune system—most important, his immune system. Of course, it would probably come out just the opposite and we would have a nearsighted, flat-footed, immune-deficient child with a very bad temper. Still, he was willing to take that risk to have a child that would be ours.

Victor admitted that he was worried that he might not be able to bond with an adopted child. He reminded me that he had always considered himself too emotionally distant for a stable marriage, much less parenthood. It might be too much to ask him to love a stranger's child. When Victor and I first fell in love, he said he had surprised himself. He thought he would have a series of short relationships with dramatic, dysfunctional women and then, over the years, grow increasingly weird, living alone, sleeping on a bare mattress on the floor in a one-room apartment piled high with books. Instead he fell in love with a woman with a close extended family and a gigantic dog who wanted all the normal things in life, a comfortable house, two kids, a garage with a station wagon, a lawn mower, and a sprinkler. He felt he had come a long way to accept these bourgeois desires, but he did not share my general love of all things helpless—puppies, injured birds, and babies. He was not the type to coo at strangers' children.

In truth, Victor is the most emotionally generous person I have ever known. It's the main reason I fell in love with him. He claims to be locked away in intellect, and it is true that his most valued possessions are his books and his camera. That suited me well. When we first met, my most valued possessions were my books and my aging Macintosh computer. One room in our small house is literally stacked floor to ceiling with our combined books, ranging from the camp to the abstruse. Friends often tell us that Victor would be their first choice for phone-a-friend on *Who Wants to Be a Millionaire*.

But behind Victor's intellectual veneer is pure gentleness. He brought my grandmother flowers when they first met. At parties he talks to the lonely person in the corner of the room. Early on he took responsibility for reminding me when to get my infusions. He asks me at night if I need to give myself a shot, and he rolls out of bed at 3 a.m. to get Tylenol if I am having a bad reaction. I was certain—even when he was not—that he would love any child we had, whether our own or adopted. After all, he had learned to love my eccentric—and most likely mentally handicapped—dog. When Roy had an upset stomach, Victor would sit with him on the front lawn in the middle of the night feeding him handfuls of grass until he felt better. When Roy decided he would no longer go on walks but had to be driven to the park, Victor gamely put him in the backseat of the car and took him there. When Roy's arthritis got so bad that he could not climb the stairs, Victor carried all 130 pounds of him so he could sleep next to our bed. He said he did these things to make me happy, but in quiet moments, when he didn't know I was watching, I saw him stroking the dog's ears and whispering to him.

I knew Victor would adapt to whatever fate determined. If we could not have our own child, he would eventually accept adoption. This gradual acceptance is probably a rite of passage for all parents of adopted children. Few choose adoption over pregnancy. But I also felt a responsibility to try to give him the biological child we both wanted. After all, it was my immune deficiency, not his. Victor had had the courage to marry someone with a chronic illness. He had accepted the inherent uncertainty of my future. He had already had to sit by his wife's hospital bed. I did not want to ask him to sacrifice having his own genetic child.

Victor was clear on one thing. Since the risk was mine, the decision was ultimately mine. He trusted my ability to make a rational choice. After all, I had the medical training to understand the possible threats to my health, or to the baby's—insofar as they could be known.

I did what research I could. After I spoke with Dr. Cunningham-Rundles, I contacted experts in the field of immune deficiency from Texas to England; none of them could give me any definite answers, but they all agreed there was no obvious risk to me or to the baby. If we had been told there was a significant risk of passing my disease on to the child, Victor and I had decided we would use a donor egg and his sperm so that the child would be at least half ours genetically. If carrying the pregnancy was dangerous, we discussed the possibility of a surrogate mother.

My parents felt these were drastic measures. They could not see the point in using a donor egg. They argued that it was not worth taxing my health with a pregnancy just to pass on 50 percent of our genes. In the end, though, Victor and I had to make the decision ourselves. And we decided we wanted our own child if at all possible.

The pain of infertility is an old one. The Bible is full of stories of barren women like Sarah and Hannah. God hears their fervent prayers, and they conceive children somewhere around the age of one hundred, which probably was thirty-four in biblical years.

It took eight more months of medical intervention for me

to get pregnant. I did not give up, even as my parents urged me to adopt, even as month after month I got cramps and blood flowed from me, even as sex became a chore, and Victor and I learned how to do it with minimal effort and even less pleasure. I took pills; I tracked my cycle. I waited. I had another piece of my uterus torn out. Victor's sperm were examined and counted and put into my body four more times.

Meanwhile everyone I knew was pregnant. My sister-in-law got pregnant her first month off the Pill. My other sister-in-law soon followed, with her second child. A colleague got pregnant accidentally while on the Pill. Kimberly, Lynn, Gail, Nona, Susan, Roberta, Samantha, Julie, and Paula got pregnant. Avery, Talia, David, Natasha, Noah, Hannah, Aidan, Liana, Charles, and Elizabeth were born. The pink line failed to appear in the window on my pregnancy tests. Once, just once, I wanted my body to work the way it was supposed to instead of this constant struggle, this heaving and pushing, just to get it up to the starting line.

Victor and I joke about how we will reply when Isabelle asks where babies come from. "Well," we will say, "first the mommy gives herself shots in the belly for two weeks. Then the mommy and daddy go to a doctor's office. The daddy goes into a room by himself and watches a movie in Swedish about a girl named Inge who decides to go hitch-hiking and meets a man named Sven." She will ask why the daddy watches a movie in Swedish. We will say the Swedish people are very good at making certain kinds of films. "Halfway through the movie, the daddy leaves the room with a cup containing a splash of whitish fluid. The doctors put the stuff in the cup into the mommy. Then the daddy gives the mommy shots in the butt with a long needle every day for two months, and then seven months later a baby is born!"

On Saturday, February 5, Victor watched about fifteen minutes of a dirty movie in a small room at the doctor's office. He came out with a small splash of fluid in a cup. The laboratory washed it and counted the sperm. I went into a room, and Dr. Hasty came in smiling. She looked at my chart. "My, my," she said. "Normally we like to see at least twenty million sperm after the washing. Victor's got sixty-three million, so that's very, very good."

I said, "He could probably impregnate the whole waiting room."

Dr. Hasty inserted a catheter into my uterus, and the washed fluid was put inside me. It took five minutes. I sat up on the edge of the examining table, and she hugged me. "Let's keep our fingers crossed," she said. "I've got a good feeling."

I shrugged. I refused to be optimistic, in order to avoid crushing disappointment.

We went home. I tried not to count the days, but I counted. I touched my breasts in the shower to see if they were tender or growing. They felt the way they always felt. Friends had catalogued the changes they felt before their pregnancy tests came back positive. I didn't feel any of them; I was not tired or ravenous or irritable or nauseated. Two weeks after the procedure, we went for the pregnancy test. I had a giant pimple on my nose, and I felt as if my ugly face matched my ugly mood. I told the doctor I wasn't pregnant. She said, "Don't be so sure."

"I don't feel anything," I said.

"What are you supposed to feel?" she asked.

"I don't know. Tired. Sick."

"It's too early for any of that. Most people don't feel anything at all."

The nurse drew my blood. Victor and I drove home in silence.

When the phone rang, I was studying for my board exams. The dog was asleep on the couch. Victor answered. I heard him say, "Tell her yourself." He handed me the phone, and I knew at that moment that I was pregnant.

Victor and I danced around the room. I was supposed to have brunch with a friend; I canceled so we could spend the day together. We were cautiously joyful. As a doctor, I also knew that almost a third of pregnancies at this stage end in miscarriage. We did not talk about names; we did not call our families.

Later that night little specks of blood appeared in my underwear. I called the doctor. She said there was nothing I could do if I was miscarrying. I just had to wait. All night long I got out of bed every fifteen minutes, trundled into the bathroom, and inspected my underwear. I counted the spots of blood. They were a brownish-red, which the doctor said was a good sign. A miscarriage would show bright red blood. I stayed home from work the next day and waited. My body felt oddly silent, the way a room feels silent when you are waiting for the phone to ring with important news. I looked at my stomach; it stared back blankly. I got out my embryology textbooks. At fourteen days of age, the baby is the size of a pencil eraser. Miscarriages that occur early in pregnancy are usually the result of chromosomal damage. If you did not miscarry, you would bear a severely deformed fetus. It is nature's way of protecting the species.

I went to the doctor's office the next day. The bleeding had stopped, and a blood test showed that the pregnancy was progressing. Dr. Hasty told me the bleeding came from the embryo implanting in the lining of the uterus. In four years of medical school, I had never heard of such a thing. Two weeks later, on an Ultrasound, we saw the fetal yolk sac. Four weeks later we saw the baby's heartbeat. In thirty-two more weeks, the doctor said, I would have a baby.

I loved being pregnant. I did not have severe morning sickness, but if I did not eat crackers first thing in the morning, wet tentacles of nausea would wave in me. I didn't mind it because it reminded me that I was pregnant. Some mornings I even waited to eat so I would feel the nausea and be reassured that there was a baby growing inside my body. My breasts grew immediately. They felt heavy in the shower, like squash growing on a vine. I would lift and wash them as if they were not a part of me. I counted the weeks as the pregnancy progressed. Victor and I read in the embryology textbooks and marked the days when the hands and feet formed, the eyes opened, the abdomen closed. Even before the pregnancy showed, I would place my hands on my belly and swear I felt a hum, a warmth, a radiance. I wanted hamburgers for dinner every night. When I was eighteen weeks pregnant, while eating a hamburger at the local pub, I felt a flutter that I realized was the baby's first movement. After that I would lie awake, waiting for her to move again. I was acutely aware that I was sharing my body. There were two of us in it. Sometimes I would press my fingers to my wrist to feel my pulse and marvel at this machine that was bringing food and oxygen to my baby.

When I was in pain, when I was sick, I hated my body, but when I was pregnant, I loved it. I loved looking at my growing belly, at my breasts, even at the love handles on my hips, the scar on my left hand, the calluses on my feet. In the shower, I could also see the warts growing, even spreading. My legs were speckled and red. When I washed under my arms, I could feel them piling up. I knew they meant that my immune system was not working right, and I worried: If it was allowing these warts to grow, what else might be brewing in me? I tried not to look at my legs, and I reminded myself that I felt well, but as the warts crept farther and farther up my arms and legs, it seemed as if we were racing: Could I deliver this baby before something terrible happened?

Then second trimester I had a series of minor infections—strep throat, a sinus infection, bronchitis—and I began to fret. Although these infections are not uncommon in pregnant women, I could not tell if they were merely bothersome illnesses or if, more gravely, they heralded a declining immune system that might leave me open to infections that could harm—or kill—both me and the baby in my belly. Certain infections during pregnancy are damaging to the fetus. They are called teratogenic infections; the word derives from the Greek word *terato*, meaning "monster," so *teratogenic* literally means "that which creates monsters."

Embryology, the study of the formation of a human baby, was fittingly the first course I took in medical school. Before we learn how the body works and then how diseases can ravage it, we must first learn where babies—and therefore bodies—come from, how two cells divide, migrate, and are transformed into a human life. My orange embryology textbook, *The Developing Human*, has a whole chapter on teratogens, which can be drugs, radiation, or infections. These agents can distort the growing fetus either by damaging chromosomes or by disturbing the normal progression of cellular development. The most infamous teratogenic drug is thalidomide, which interfered with the movement and division of cells so that children were born with flippers instead of arms and in some cases with no legs or arms at all. There are other terrible stories from recent human history, like the epidemic of children born with cerebral palsy, severe mental retardation, and blindness caused by mercury in the waters in the bay of Minimata, Japan. Radiation causes chromosomal abnormalities that can result in a wide range of horrible genetic diseases, with such deformities as heads the size of plums or watermelons or brains only big enough to sustain breathing.

Doctors know very well how much can go wrong in pregnancy. In medical school, we learn every possible horrible thing that can happen to a fetus, from exposure to drugs or radiation or simply from a fluke of nature that we are powerless to prevent. We study pictures of children with banana-shaped heads, with lobster-claw hands, with open abdomens that spill out the contents of the body. We learn about children whose kidneys fail, whose nerves fray, who are confined to wheelchairs where they can do nothing but drool and shake with seizures; children with bones as brittle as twigs, with hearts that pump backward, and with withered lungs. A friend who is not a doctor told me the worst part of her amniocentesis happened before the test, when she sat with the doctor in her office and was told all the things the test might discover. I told her, "For a doctor, the worst part is knowing all the things the test *can't* find out." A routine amniocentesis can pick up about twenty genetic diseases; there are thousands more that go undetected, devastating diseases from muscular dystrophy to Cockayne's syndrome, whose victims die by age six with the withered faces and wrinkled skin of ninety-year-olds.

In the course of my education, I have seen a child born with only a brain stem, the back of her head almost sliced away so that her skull looked like half a globe. Since birth the child could do little beyond breathing; a tube in her stomach fed her. She was almost two years old when I met her. She had never spoken and never would speak; she was blind, since she lacked the part of the brain needed for vision. Her useless eyes jiggled in her head. She would never see the world, never smell, never smile. I saw a child with severe Down's syndrome whose heart was visible, pounding through his thin chest, swollen to three times its normal size. I saw kids with cystic fibrosis gasping for air, trundling their green oxygen tanks behind them on red wagons, kids with muscular dystrophy propped up with metal rods in their backs. I cared for a child with adrenal leukodystrophy whose mother brought him to the hospital to watch him die. He was eighteen months old.

In some ways, it's a wonder doctors choose to have children at all. We have to remind ourselves that the vast majority of babies are born healthy, that these diseases are rare, and that there is no reason to suspect we will be any less lucky than anyone else. Still, we tend to be more anxious during our pregnancies. A friend who is married to a pediatrician told me that his wife was convinced the baby was having seizures every time it had a case of hiccups. A pregnant resident I knew refused to go see a child with a rare and terrible skin disease who was transferred to our hospital, even though we were told to see the baby as part of our education. She said it would give her nightmares. It was wise of her not to go. The baby was encased in a layer of angry red skin so thick that her mouth would not close; it was fixed open in a permanent, mute scream, and her eyelids had turned inside out so that her eyes were filled with red flesh.

I shared the same concerns as other female doctors who become pregnant, but I also had concerns specific to my condition. Four main infections are known to cause deformed babies: syphilis, rubella, cytomegalovirus, and toxoplasmosis. Every woman is tested for these diseases at her first prenatal visit. In the case of syphilis, treatment prior to conception or early in pregnancy and avoidance of new infection prevents the problem altogether. Most women are immune to rubella, or German measles, through vaccination. The cytomegalovirus is a member of the herpes virus family that is transmitted through feces and is common in young children and AIDS patients. Often women have been exposed and become immune to it without ever having been aware of an infection. Women who turn out not to have antibodies to cytomegalovirus must be careful to avoid changing diapers on other children and must avoid exposure to immune-compromised patients, especially AIDS patients. Toxoplasmosis is caused by a parasite that is found in cat feces and uncooked meat. It is fairly rare in the United States, though not uncommon in Europe. Many women have no immunity to toxoplasmosis, but the chances of exposure are low. Pregnant women who own cats are advised to have someone else change the litter box.

Since I don't make good antibodies, I was worried that I would not have immunity to rubella or cytomegalovirus, particularly the latter since it is the form of virus I seem uniquely unable to fight. My first round of blood tests showed that I had antibodies to rubella and cytomegalovirus. There was no way to know if the antibodies I had were made by my own body or if they came from my monthly infusions, but it was most likely the latter. Antibodies don't last forever in the body. They decompose after four to six weeks, and in a healthy person they are replaced by a newly minted set. In my case, I borrow a fresh set every four weeks, but the four-week interval is an approximation. A healthy body can tell that an antibody has disappeared and will automatically make more to take its place. A normal woman who has immunity to rubella will always have immunity to rubella. If I stopped my infusions, I would probably lose my immunity. If I were late with one infusion, there is also a possibility that my immunity would be lost. It was essential that I continue my infusions during the pregnancy, increasing the amount I received as I gained weight.

I understood all these basic principles before I got pregnant. I had been reassured that as long as I received my infusions, I should be safe. I would not have tried to become pregnant if there was a high risk that I would bear a deformed or sick child. But somehow, as soon as I became pregnant, these reassurances thinned and crumbled, and I was overcome with anxiety. The warts were continuing to spread on my legs and arms. Every night when I undressed, I saw them creeping over me. I wore long sleeves and long pants, so I still appeared healthy to my patients and my coworkers, but I knew that if I walked into the office of a doctor who did not know I had an immune deficiency, he would immediately order an AIDS test.

My job exposed me to contagious diseases on a daily basis. The blood of an AIDS patient splashed on my arm. There was a flood in the clinic, and raw sewage spilled over our examining tables and microscopes, potentially exposing me to cytomegalovirus. As a medical student, I cared for a child with congenital cytomegalovirus. Her name was

Nicole. She was eleven years old, and she had black hair and big black eyes with long eyelashes that were always half shut so she looked sleepy and dreamy all the time. She was all knotted up from brain damage, and her pink gums were so swollen from the medicine she had to take to control her seizures, they seemed to bubble out of her mouth. She couldn't eat, so she had a tube in her stomach for feeding. She drooled. Her mother combed her long hair and turned her in bed; she was heavy, and it was not easy. Her parents had divorced, and they took care of her in alternate shifts. Her mother lived with her in a trailer with a set of IV poles to deliver the child's food and medications, a nebulizer to help her breathe when she had an asthma attack, a closet full of pills. Her father worked in construction. He wore T-shirts that advertised automotive parts and stroked her hair gently. She was their only child.

I called Dr. Cunningham-Rundles. She tried to calm me down. She explained that tests had been done on the levels of cytomegalovirus in gamma globulin. I should have immunity for up to six months after an infusion. She said if I was worried, I could go ahead and get an infusion right away. I scheduled the infusion for the next day.

My fear of congenital cytomegalovirus was succeeded by my fear of toxoplasmosis. Walking the dog one night, I reached down to pull a stick out of his mouth. It was covered in cat feces. I ran home and washed my hands. Then I called a friend who is an expert on infectious diseases. He reassured me that my chances of infection were very low. Toxoplasmosis, he said, is very rare in the southeastern United States. Only 4 percent of cats will shed the parasite and at one point only in their lives. Still, if I was worried, I could get a blood test. I got the test. It showed no evidence of infection, but I would have to wait another month for a follow-up test to be sure.

I was waking up at night and pulling textbooks off the shelf to look up exactly how cytomegalovirus and toxoplasmosis damage a child. Mental retardation, big heads, small heads, deafness, blindness. If I got HIV, I would probably progress rapidly to AIDS because my immune system could not contain the virus. I would die quickly. If I got cytomegalovirus, both my baby and I would probably have severe forms of the disease. I would wake my husband to inform him of these facts. He would remind me that I had been told not to worry. "Worrying," he said, "is not good for the baby either." He would go back to sleep, and I would crouch in the bathroom for hours with the door closed so the light wouldn't wake him, reading my textbooks and counting the ever-increasing warts on my legs and arms.

When I was sixteen weeks pregnant, I was removing a cancerous mole from an HIV-positive patient when I felt a prick on my finger from the hook I was using to pull the edges of the skin together. I was wearing two layers of gloves to protect myself, and there was no evidence that the sharp end of the hook had broken the glove. I was pregnant and did not want to take an antiviral medication to prevent HIV transmission in a situation where I appeared to have no exposure. I dismissed the whole incident until two weeks later, when I developed what I later realized was a sinus infection. I panicked, thinking that the infection meant I had contracted HIV. In the early stages of HIV infection, patients can develop severe headache, fever, swollen lymph nodes, and a rash. I had a bad headache and a fever, with tenderness over the frontal sinuses in the forehead—classic signs, I knew, of a sinus infection, not of HIV infection. I would have dismissed anyone else's worries with absolute confidence, but I could not dismiss my own. I called my obstetrician; I even called another physician who is an expert on HIV. They both reassured me that there was nothing to worry about. But I could not accept their reassurances. I brought home the instrument that had pricked me. I tested it again and again on my skin to make sure it would not break the skin. It never drew blood, no matter how hard I pressed. The worry would recede for a few days and return. I slept with the instrument by my bed and would wake up in the middle of the night and obsessively test again and again.

I finally went to see a psychiatrist. He told me I was having panic attacks and should consider taking Prozac. I said I would prefer not to, since the long-term effects of Prozac on fetal development are unknown. He nodded. Then he said, "I think you're anxious because you're off your interferon."

I looked at him, confused. "But interferon wouldn't protect me from HIV or toxoplasmosis. Maybe it would help fight cytomegalovirus, but I'm not even sure of that. That isn't the reason I'm so anxious," I said with certainty.

"Then what is?"

I thought a minute. His office was bare but for a government-issue desk with a plastic tray holding patients' charts. "I'm anxious," I said. I repeated, "I'm anxious . . ." There were no windows. There weren't even any pictures on the wall. I got the sense he'd just moved in. "Maybe I'm anxious," I said, "because I'm bringing a child into the world, and I'm not sure I'll be here to see her grow up. I can't even get life insurance. I applied. They turned me down. They don't think I'm worth the risk. I'm anxious because I'm bringing a life into this world, and I may already have damaged her. She may be sick because of me." I started to cry.

"That would explain why someone might panic, wouldn't it?"

Those of us who live with chronic illnesses often teeter closer to the fear of death because we are more acutely aware of the fragility of our bodies. As a new body grew inside of me, I was aware not only of the vulnerability of my body but also of hers. And I worried, for me and for her.

Once I had this insight, I didn't stop worrying. In fact, at that moment, I knew that I might as well just start setting an extra place at the table for worry. It had moved in and was never leaving. My parents say worry is at the heart of raising children, and with each successive stage of your child's life, you take your worries to the dealership and trade them in for a whole new set. Once she is born with ten fingers and ten toes, you worry that she will get sick. You avoid children with runny noses; you take her temperature. You memorize the telephone number of your pediatrician. As the months pass, you worry that she will never stand, and then when she stands, you worry that she will fall down. She starts to walk, and then you worry that she will stick her hand in an outlet or drown in a swimming pool or drink a bottle of Clorox. She reaches the age at which she knows not to drink a bottle of Clorox, and you worry that she will drink a bottle of alcohol or get in a car with someone who has drunk a bottle of alcohol. She takes a trip to Europe and her postcards get lost in the mail, and you do not know where she is, and you worry. You worry that she was gored to death while running with the bulls in Pamplona or has fallen in love with a Frenchman and is never coming home. She comes home, and she gets married, and she gets pregnant, and you worry that she will die while delivering the baby. She delivers the baby, and then you worry about her *and* the baby.

When Isabelle was born, all I could say was "Oh, my God. Oh, my God." Those three words, diminished by overuse, were just the right words for an experience that was the closest I have ever felt to being in the presence of the divine. The child was warm, with waxy, deep pink skin, the color and feel of a tulip petal. Her tiny eyes blinked and squinted at me. Swirls of black hair were wet and clinging to her head. She did not cry. I held her in my arms, then pressed her to my chest, where she could hear the same heartbeat she had heard for the past nine months, now muffled and distant, and my voice, no longer obscured by the whooshing of blood and the beating of her heart and mine. "Hello, Isabelle." She turned her eyes to my voice. She was looking for me. She was helpless, and I was the one who must protect her. Her hands were the size of quarters; I could cover her whole head with my hand.

The nurse took her to get her cleaned up. She commented, "She's a little one."

Jacqui was busy delivering the placenta and extracting blood from the umbilical cord. She told me, "You didn't even tear. It was a perfect delivery."

When the nurse brought the baby back to me, I guided her mouth to my breast, and she sucked. I could not stop looking at her. She was so small but so perfect; there were little creases over her knuckles, swirls on her finger pads. I could feel the round bones of her wrists, the flat bones of her shoulders. She breathed and cried and rested her head on my chest. I had waited for a long time to hold her, but I felt as if I had been holding her for centuries. After a while, the nurse gently told me that they had to take the baby to the nursery to be weighed and measured. Victor went with her. My parents left to call everyone they had ever met.

The nurses brought a wheelchair to transfer me to my

room on the postpartum unit. There was blood on my hospital gown. In the room, a new nurse came in. She told me she would draw up a sitz bath. She handed me a fresh ice pack and a squeeze bottle and told me to squirt my vagina with warm water every time I went to the bathroom. She gave me a stool softener and some Motrin. I wondered where the baby was.

The nurse wrote the number for the nursery on the wall. I called them and asked for my baby. They told me she was still cold from her bath. Victor came and told me the baby was small, only five pounds three ounces and eighteen inches long. She was even smaller than my niece, who was five and a half pounds and born two weeks early.

When my mother heard the news, she said, "That *is* small."

I didn't think much of her size at first. I was just so happy to have her. My parents went home. Victor left for Federal Express to send the package containing the umbilical cord blood to Duke University in North Carolina, where it would be frozen and stored in case Isabelle or I ever needed it for a bone marrow transplant. I had been advised that it was unlikely she would ever need it, but it might be useful for me. The nursery brought Isabelle Rachel back to me, and I picked her up and let her nurse. I flipped on the television. The East Coast polls were closed, and the networks were already predicting winners. I turned the TV to the "new mother channel" and watched a lesson on bathing your newborn and taking care of the umbilical cord. Isabelle had a black charred stump where the cord used to be, where my blood had flowed into her. She fell asleep, and I swaddled her and held her next to me, and I fell asleep, too.

The next day was a blur of phone calls and visitors and sitz baths and trying to learn to nurse the baby. My parents were in and out. I had forgotten about the election, and it was almost surprising to see the television news full of stories of Bush and Gore instead of the arrival of my daughter. My brother Jonathan, who is a political journalist, called me from Gore headquarters, where he had been up all night covering the election returns. There was no winner yet in the presidential election. Florida, it turned out, was too close to call. They had to have a recount. Victor couldn't watch the television. Instead, we watched our beautiful, sleepy baby. Sleepy. She was very sleepy. I never knew that newborns sleep most of the first two days of their lives. The nurses told me to squeeze her feet to get her to wake up to nurse. She preferred sleeping. The visitors all commented on how small she was.

The pediatrician came to see her in the hospital. "She is perfectly healthy," she told me. "Just small. She'll catch up."

I told the pediatrician, "I might drive you crazy because I am a doctor, and I also have a congenital immune deficiency. Everyone says there's very little—or no—chance of her being affected, but I'm going to be a little paranoid."

The doctor laughed. "Well, just one of those things—either being a doctor or having a medical condition—would be bad enough." She reminded me, "Kids get viruses."

"I know. It's different when I get a virus."

We looked down at the tiny baby in the bassinet. "Try not to worry," the doctor said. "She can go home with you tomorrow."

The next day, when a nurse said, "That's a little one. Was she early?" I burst into tears. I realized that she was, by definition, small for gestational age. I wanted to know why, what happened. I was suddenly scared. I was sobbing. The nurse told me that I was just upset because of hormonal fluctuations. "But she's so little," I said.

"Some are little. Some are big," she answered.

"She's small for gestational age."

The lactation consultant told me I might have to supplement with formula because she was so small.

My mother told me not to worry. Jacqui told me not to worry. She's perfectly healthy, they all said. Another doctor stopped by, took one look at her, and asked, "Was she early?"

I started crying again.

The baby was crying. She was hungry, and my milk hadn't come in. No one was with me. My mother was getting the house ready for us, shopping and cooking. Victor was having the car seat installed and picking up his parents at the airport. Isabelle and I were both in abject despair. The nurse came in. She took the baby from me and calmed her down. She told me she was going to send the baby to the nursery so I could sleep, but I couldn't sleep. The room was suddenly quiet without the baby. I stared at the ceiling. I ran through the differential diagnosis of babies who are small for gestational age: smoking, drug abuse, alcoholism—okay, none of those. Transplacental infection, a distinct risk for me—we had tested to make sure I was immune, but what if the immunity waxed and waned with my infusions? She looked normal—ears, eyes, head all proportionate—but some birth defects don't show up until children are a year old, or even later, when they start school. Maybe my having a child was like sheltering someone from a storm in a ramshackle house, maybe my body wasn't strong enough to protect her. She was only two days old, and already I had failed her. I cried some more.

Forty-eight hours after delivery, as mandated by my insurance company, I went home. Victor came to get me. The nurse loaded up a deluxe wheelchair with the flowers and banners that had been delivered, the CD player, the massage oil we never used. An orderly wheeled me to the front of the hospital, and we waited for Victor to bring the car around. To my shock, another woman in a wheelchair was waiting there, too, also cuddling a baby. It was startling to suddenly realize that on the day Isabelle was born, a day that changed my life completely, hundreds of other babies were born, and hundreds of other lives were changed. The other baby looked gigantic compared to Isabelle. The mother said, "Oh, yours is so cute and tiny." Tears leaked out. Her baby boy weighed ten pounds. I didn't want to tell her how much Isabelle weighed. Compared with her child, Isabelle looked like a toy.

We put our tiny baby into the car seat. It swallowed her up. She flopped to one side, and I had to hold her head in place so she wouldn't fold back up into herself and disappear in a terrible sort of magic trick. Outside the hospital, the world was unchanged. Cars whizzed up and down Peachtree Street. The remains of a half-drunk latte were in the cup holder. Christmas wreaths hung from telephone poles, even though, as usual for Georgia, it was too warm for Christmas. My little girl was tiny, and I didn't know why. I didn't know if some terrible fate had already been woven for her, if some tragic mistake on my part, careless or unknowing, had doomed her to a painful future. I wanted to protect her, and I didn't know how.

When we were all in the labor room—Victor, my parents and myself—Victor had casually commented, "The last time we were all in a hospital together, Jamie had the parotid infection." I knew in a rush the awful suffering that my illness has brought on my parents. I was their tiny baby once; they held me as I was holding my newborn child, and they had hopes for me and dreams that did not include me whimpering in pain or scared of dying. I felt what it was for my husband and my parents to stand around that hospital bed and want more than anything in the world to be able to help me—and to be utterly powerless, to be reminded so sharply that human beings can really offer each other no protection at all. Love is a very thin veil to cast over each other, easily, easily pierced.

At home, my tiny baby slept all the time. She turned yellow. Visitors were scared to hold her because they had never seen a child so small. When I held her on my lap to burp her, I could feel the sharp edges of her shoulder blades, unusually prominent, as if, until recently, wings had sprouted there. I was certain I was starving her to death and that she was slowly disappearing before my eyes. The day after I came home, I went to the pediatrician's office in a panic. "There's less and less of her every day," I said. "And she won't eat."

The pediatrician told me I had to be mean. I could not let her sleep. I had to put a cold washcloth on her face. I had to scratch the bottoms of her feet and squeeze her hands. I had to make her eat. Was she eating? I could not tell. Sometimes she clamped onto my breast and pulled so I felt like one of those strange people on TV specials who hang from ropes by their nipples. Sometimes she took her tiny fists, the size of quarters, and pushed me away. Mostly she slept, no matter what I did. I ran to the lactation consultant. She said, "Oh, the baby's small for gestational age. Do you have any idea why?"

I shook my head no and tried not to cry. Of course I had

many ideas why. All the worries I'd had during pregnancy were flooding me. At night I lay in a bed drenched with worries, a soupy mess of them that I waded through as I lay awake, waiting for my baby to cry. Which of those many diseases had sneaked in through my body and seized my baby?

The lactation consultant watched me feed the baby and said I was doing just fine.

"But she's so small," I said.

"She won't stay that way."

"How can you be sure?" I asked. It looked to me like she was evaporating.

She weighed the baby. "She's gained five ounces since you brought her home from the hospital. She's doing just fine."

I looked at the baby skeptically.

At five in the morning, it dawned on me that she might have toxoplasmosis. I woke my husband up, sobbing. "Toxoplasmosis," I informed him in the predawn darkness, "can be asymptomatic at birth. It can present with just low birth weight."

He sat up in bed, blinking. He is almost blind without his glasses, and so I almost never see his face without them on. He looked bare and vulnerable. His blue eyes were small and lost. "What difference does it make if she does?" he asked.

He had already dealt with so much, choosing to marry and share his life with someone whose future was so uncertain, who gave herself shots at night and spent weeks in the hospital and who could not even buy life insurance. Victor gets mad at me when I forget to give myself a shot or am reluctant to call a doctor for fear of my complaints seeming trivial, and I knew at that moment, knew sharply and deeply, where that anger came from.

I have been a patient, cared for by doctors and worried over by my family. I have been a doctor myself, trying to ease the suffering of my patients and comfort their families. But I have been fortunate to have two healthy parents, healthy brothers, and a husband who is flat-footed and near-sighted and prone to sunburn but otherwise just fine. I have never had to stand by and watch a loved one suffer the way my family has stood by me. Now I had opened myself to the possibility of such pain. He turned his face toward my voice. "She's our baby. We'll deal with it." He reached for my hand. He was trying to hold on to me. I was trying to hold on to Isabelle.

Healthy people can get life and disability insurance. I cannot. An actuary somewhere has looked at my medical records and decided that I am more likely than the average young woman to experience a prolonged illness or an early death. I already knew this. Most people live in fear of some terrible event changing their lives, the death of a loved one or a serious illness. For the chronically ill, this terrible event has already happened, and we have been let in on an amazing secret: You survive. You adapt, and your life changes, but in the end you go on, with whatever compromises you have been forced to make, whatever losses you have been forced to endure. You learn to balance your fears with the simple truth that you must go on living. But the fact that people buy life insurance tells me that my fears are not so different from the fears of others. We are all, to some extent, aware of our mortality. After each holiday weekend, we are told how many people died in accidents. We pass a line of cars with their lights on, trailing a hearse, and we know that they are going to a funeral. At some point, our parents stop telling us that someone has gone away on a long vacation and start to explain what it means to die, and from then on, we know that someday this fate will befall us, and it will befall the ones we love, and each of us, miraculously, learns to live with this fact.

All the worrying in the world cannot prepare you for the terrible things that will happen. My parents worried, and their children did get sick. When he was five, Jonathan fell down the cement stairs behind the house that led to the woodpile and cut his head; he still has the scar in the shape of an arrow. When I was seven, I broke my wrist while playing on the jungle gym. When he was eight, Jonathan got his foot caught in another boy's bicycle wheel, and his ankle snapped in two. When he was thirteen, Mark broke his wrist skiing; at sixteen he wrecked the car. When I was fifteen, I got shingles, then strep throat, then strep throat again. I grew warts all over my body. Then I couldn't hear, and then a doctor told my parents I had cancer. Then I didn't have cancer, but I had something else, something that would stay with me all my life, that might or might not kill me but would never be cured. All children will get cuts and bruises, sore throats and fevers, but some of them will get much worse—leukemia, a brain tumor, an immune deficiency. Some will die in a car accident, and some will drown. Here's the tricky part: No one knows which ones.

My parents have accepted and dealt with these things one by one. My mother had three children by the time she was twenty-three years old. She tells me she had no idea what it would mean to be a parent. She says if anyone really knew how hard it is to raise a child, there would be no parents. You can't measure love any more than you can measure pain, and so there is no way to know if the joy your children bring you is worth the worry and the heartache, the wrenching heartache, you feel every time you see them sick. I know that my parents have felt great sorrow because they had me. Holding my child now, I am closer to knowing what it must have been like for my mother to sit by my hospital bed and stroke my hair while I begged to be allowed to die, to escape the pain that had seized me. So far my child has cried for hunger, fatigue, loneliness, and—briefly but sharply and with horror—from pain, when a nurse plunged a long needle into her leg, vaccinating her. Her cry tore me, even though I knew where her pain came from, and I knew it would end. My mother did not know those things. She watched illness descend mysteriously on her child and envelop her. I cannot imagine how she has survived those moments, except for the odd grace of having no choice but to survive.

At the time of this writing, Isabelle is a healthy five-month-old baby. She did not have toxoplasmosis or any of the other diseases I feared. She is growing and eating and laughing. She has learned to roll over from her back to her stomach, though she can't yet roll back the other way, and it frustrates her. She'll spend five minutes struggling on her stomach and then cry for one of us to come fix the problem. We think she's quite a flirt. She's an easy smiler. She has her grandparents—both sets—wrapped around her pudgy hand. And her hand is pudgy. She's still small but is growing appropriately for her size, and the doctors all tell us she's thriving. The dog hasn't acknowledged her existence yet, but over the last week she's suddenly become aware of him, and she'll watch him as he lumbers about the room. I have recovered from delivery and am back on interferon injections. The warts on my legs have started to melt away, and my lymph nodes are shrinking. There do not seem to have been any negative consequences to my year off medication, although it may be too soon to tell, and we may never know. If I develop lymphoma in the future, perhaps this year off interferon opened the door; perhaps not. It is best not to know. The uncertainty of our existence has crippled men and women wiser than I, but it is probably true that the only thing worse than not knowing the future would be knowing it and being unable to alter its course.

I look down at the tiny creature in my arms. Already you can tell that she has her father's eyes, blue and almond shaped, with a pale dusting of hair for eyebrows. Her lips are a perfect pink bow. Her hand is no longer smaller than my thumb, but I can easily put her entire foot in my mouth. When something startles her, both arms fly into the air. I don't know what life has in store for her. Will she be healthy until she is a teenager, as I was, and then suddenly become plagued with mysterious illnesses? Maybe by then there will be a cure for this disease, or at least a name. Will she love to read, as I do, or will she be an athlete? Will she marry her first love? Will she ride horses, paint pictures, love snow, get into the college of her choice, live in an old Victorian house near the ocean, live in an apartment in New York City, a log cabin, a houseboat? And as she lives, what pains will be visited on her body, broken arms and cuts that need stitches, the flu, poison ivy, or terrible diseases that eat away the nerves and the brain—could she one day shake with Parkinson's or wander like a child lost at school, disoriented by Alzheimer's? Could her heart fail her and her lungs fill with water? Could a tumor grow in her breast; could a stray bullet find her; could she fall from a great height, ski off a cliff, get lost in the woods and shiver with cold? All these things might happen—or none of them. A mother prays that the baby she holds will grow and walk and talk, love and marry and hold children of her own. And then, late in life, wrinkles will creep into her skin, and her eyes will dim, and she'll wear silver reading glasses around her neck and always need a sweater, even in summer, and then one night, a long, long time from now, when I am gone, she will go to bed, with pictures of children and grandchildren on the nightstand, watch TV, fall asleep, and not wake up. All of my child's life stretches before her, with its infinite paths, some leading to joy and others to tears, but we have no map, and we can't know where she's going until she gets there.

During the nine months of my pregnancy, men and women have died. I myself have cared for young women who have left motherless children behind. Although I hope to live a long life and to see my child grow up, I may not be so fortunate. This misfortune, I know as a doctor, can befall anyone, but the odds are less in my favor than for most other women I know. I don't know those odds, though. No one does. Because of my illness, I find myself reduced to and daily confronted with the fundamental blindness of humanity. My illness has forced me to make consciously the choice that the greater part of humanity makes without thinking each day, to soldier forward in our ignorance.

I hear Isabelle laughing in the nursery. She loves to look at herself in the mirror, though I am fairly sure she does not realize that the face she sees is her own. It is just a face, with two eyes and a smile, a human being who smiles back at her. She cackles with unbridled delight at the sight of that face, and I laugh with her, with no less joy. It is spring again, and my body affords me the sight of daffodils and the scent of early blossoms on the trees, the sounds of birds

talking as they build their nests and of my daughter laughing, and crying when she's hungry, the feeling of my husband's hand on my shoulder and the taste of my child's skin,
slightly salty and soapy from the bath. My body affords me
these pleasures for a limited time only, but what great pleasures they are. And how I love them.

ACKNOWLEDGMENTS

I owe thanks to the many people who have contributed to the writing of this book. My editor, Becky Saletan, shared my vision of the book from the start; she is a patient teacher and a cherished friend. My agent, Elaine Markson, encouraged me through the long years of writing and residency, pregnancy and motherhood.

I cannot acknowledge all the physicians and nurses who have cared for and educated me, but a few standouts must be mentioned, in particular Dr. Charlotte Cunningham-Rundles. Her knowledge of immunology is matched only by her compassion and patience. Through the years, she has guided me not only in my career but in many of the choices

I make in life; she has answered countless questions and e-mails, and has become my friend and mentor as well as my physician. She is a role model for everything I do in medicine.

At Mount Sinai Hospital, the infusion room nurses, Sarah Martin and Monica Reiter-Wong, have been models of both empathy and humor. At Emory University, Helmut Albrecht, Bill Grist, Gerald Gussack, Tom Heffner, Ira Horowitz, Bob Swerlick, Charlotte Williams, Yuri Hairston, Kevin Schreffler, Anita Germaneso, and Jane Wood have all at times cared for me and taught me with great skill and wisdom, challenging me to think not only about the workings of the body but also about the goals and limits of medicine.

I have had the good fortune to know many patients, as both a doctor and a friend. Jane Cooper inspires me with her boundless love of life and literature. Patsy Butterworth showed me how to feel joy in the face of sorrow. Kimberly Williams and the participants on the Immune_Deficiency list-serv have shared their lives, their compromises, and their triumphs with me.

I cannot begin to thank my parents and my two brothers for their tireless love. When I am well, we share the joys of life, and when I am ill, they give me a reason to endure. My wonderful daughter, Isabelle, has deepened my understanding of what it is to love, bringing me more joy than she can know. And finally, this book would not have been written without the insight and inspiration of my husband, Victor Balaban. He was the first to suggest I explore the dual role I play as doctor and patient, and he has guided me through countless writings and rewritings, patiently offering criticism and suggestions, and supporting me through frustration and fatigue. He is the most brilliant, courageous, and creative man I have ever known.